Miracle
Power
to
Overcome
Illness

IRH Press

BOOKS
IRH PRESS
New York

ISBN: 978-1-958655-17-7
Cover Image: eugenesergeev/PIXTA

Printed in Canada

First Edition

HEALING THROUGH
FAITH

The
Miracle
Power
to
Overcome
Illness

EL CANTARE

RYUHO OKAWA

IRH PRESS

Contents

CHAPTER ONE

The Miracle Power
to Overcome Illness

CHAPTER TWO

Question and Answer Sessions on Illnesses

Afterword

Preface

Of all worries and distress, illness weighs a great amount on people's minds. When people are healthy, their desires for worldly status, fame, and power will only get stronger. But in times of illness, they will become preoccupied with physical pain and suffering and will be consumed by various negative thoughts, such as financial worries and concerns over the trouble they may cause to their family and society. They will only wish for small things for themselves. Their minds will mostly be filled with very humble wishes like "I want to walk freely," "I want to go to the bathroom on my own," or "I want to bathe one more time." Former elites who graduated from top-flight universities, or former athletes, for example, would probably suffer more by feeling how significantly they have fallen from grace.

You need to pursue the Middle Way between your work and your life. You must also awaken to the Truth that people can only realize how important kindness is by going through suffering and sadness. To think deeply about the meaning of Illness and Aging is also an important work in life for people in their middle age and older. Please be aware of this.

Ryuho Okawa
Master & CEO of Happy Science Group
February 13, 2018

CHAPTER

1

The Miracle Power
to Overcome Illness

Originally recorded in Japanese on June 30, 2016
at the Special Lecture Hall of Happy Science in Japan
and later translated into English.

The Factors That Make Miracles Happen

Problems surrounding illness are one of the major fields in religion, so I believe I should talk about it every now and again.

Recently, I conducted two spiritual messages, one from the founder of a Japanese religious group called Seicho-No-Ie (Masaharu Taniguchi), and another from the guardian spirit of the religion's third leader. During its founder's age, their promotion was often along the lines of, "You can cure illnesses by reading our books," and people have actually recovered on some occasions. But ever since the third leader succeeded as president, materialistic ideas became prominent, making the religion more worldly, and their opinions started becoming journalistic. Strangely, people hardly get better from their illness anymore. What's more, the third president often denies the founder's teachings. There is nothing wrong in him criticizing the teachings to point out the wrongful ones. But it seems to me that he is doing so because compared to when the founder was the president, fewer people are recovering from illnesses. So he can't resist but criticize the teachings.

For a miracle to happen, it is crucial to understand the power of the mind, the workings of the Spirit World, the workings of angels, and the power of God. Miracles rarely occur to people who do not understand these factors.

However, it is a fact that many people have experienced a miracle but do not realize that it happened. They only think that such an incident is a mere coincidence or it occurred by chance. At times, religion also teaches about how to live wisely in a worldly sense. That is what makes things complicated. Worldly wisdom is important, of course, but as long as you are undergoing religious training, you must know that you are a spiritual entity and deepen this awareness, year after year.

The Mindsets and Habits Necessary to Prevent Illnesses

Adopt good eating habits and a good lifestyle

Illness is something that everyone usually experiences at least once or twice in their life. Very few people can live out their lives without ever falling ill. Some people dislike going to the doctors and hospitals, so they may leave this world without knowing that they are ill. But when people go to a hospital, doctors will usually label any kind of symptom they may have with a particular illness. That is why illnesses are believed to exist. Let's say a person dies from what used to be called natural death in old times. If he or she was at the hospital, doctors nowadays will most probably label the cause of death with a certain disease. In this sense, almost everyone experiences illness in their lifetime.

Nowadays, scientific research has advanced a lot and various medical treatments and medicines have been developed. In the old days, it was often said that illnesses came from the mind. But this idea alone is no longer enough to cure all illnesses today.

During and after World War II, when food was scarce, simple things were surprisingly effective. For instance, in the late 1950s around the time when I was born, I knew many people who suffered from tuberculosis. It was called *rougai* in Japanese during the Edo Period (17th-19th century) and was well-known as a deadly disease. It was often found in people who suffered from malnutrition. So, at times when food was scarce, even eggs worked like medicine. Sometimes, sick people recovered surprisingly well after they ate just an egg. Likewise, milk would energize them and meat, which was a rare food at the time, was also effective.

In this way, people can get better by consuming what they lack in their diet or adopting new lifestyle habits. These are times when logical thinking or a worldly perspective can come in handy. Just as some nutrients are necessary for plants to grow and not wither, some things are necessary for humans to live.

Have a strong will and the will to improve yourself

On the topic of illness, we need to think about the following. First is prevention, in other words, taking necessary measures beforehand. Second is the efforts you need to make while you are ill to recover from it. And third is the precautions or the lifestyle you must lead until the very last day of your life after you recover from an illness. In terms of time frames, these are the three phases we must consider.

Let me first talk about prevention. Modern medicine is mostly based on statistics. They usually collect data from patients with the same illness from around the country. They then identify any figures that are abnormal or are off the average compared to the healthy population and consider those factors as the cause of the illness. This is what usually underlies the treatment procedure.

In this way, having eating habits or a lifestyle that is quite different from an average person may make you susceptible to certain illnesses. By trying to fix your habit so you are within normal standards, you can eliminate the cause of potential illness.

This is by no means a miracle, but maintaining a healthy mental condition and lifestyle is not so easy to do. You need a strong will to lead a regular life and to do so, you must have a strong aspiration or the will to improve yourself. I believe this is, in a sense, an act of giving back to God.

Why does your view on life change
after experiencing a serious illness?

It is often said that your view on life will change after experiencing a serious illness. That is because, by experiencing a difficult time in your life, people will, for the first time, feel grateful for the things they took for granted when they were healthy and strong. I am not recommending people to become ill, but there are many things you are unaware of when you are healthy.

For example, if you become a wheelchair user, you will realize how wonderful it is to be able to walk on your own two feet. When you think about it, being able to walk on two legs, in itself, is quite an amazing thing. Most animals walk on four legs, which is very stable. Even with vehicles, it is hard to drive them with only two wheels. You would at least want three wheels to make it more stable, with one at the front and two at the back, for example. It takes a lot of skills to be able to drive a two-wheel vehicle. In the same way, standing on two legs is challenging. Given how small human soles are, bearing all the body weight and maintaining a good balance to walk must be a tough job.

While it is true that acquired traits cannot be inherited, it is also not entirely true. Human beings have acquired the ability to walk on two feet, but I believe this is a result of their fundamental desire to do so, and this ability has been inherited for generations. When standing on two feet, each foot bears a considerable amount of weight—dozens of kilograms or pounds. So, just being able to go about a day standing on two feet is an amazing thing.

Drinking too much fluid will lead to water poisoning

In the desert, you would suffer if you cannot drink water, but drinking too much of it can make you ill. In civilized countries, people living in big cities sometimes become ill by consuming too much water. This is often called the "CEO's disease" in Japan. If CEOs constantly keep on drinking what they are served throughout the day, they will have too much water in their bodies. What is more, because they work in modernized city buildings, their bodies are used to not sweating, so their system could be weak at discharging the water. This can result in retaining excess water in the body, which can lead to water poisoning. There are many CEOs who develop this kind of illness. The more they are attended by their employees, the more they become susceptible to this disease.

In terms of diet, you may think you are eating well and are eating high-quality food, but this can also lead you to excessive water intake. For example, when you eat a lot of salty food, you would also drink a lot of water. Salty food will make you thirsty, so you will drink more water. This can make you have excess body fluid, which can also make you susceptible to illness.

Another problem is an unbalanced diet. An unbalanced diet can change your body composition, so if it goes to an extreme, you will naturally become ill.

Be wary of extreme dieting methods

There are various dieting methods in the world that seem medically correct, but you need to be wary of the extreme ones. For example, if you are recommended the one-meal-a-day diet, it may sound appealing to you because it saves money and makes you think you can slim down. But eating only one meal a day can be somewhat harmful to your body.

Another diet is the two-meals-a-day diet, which will indeed make you lose weight. But if people like sumo wrestlers use this method, they will sometimes gain weight instead. If they train in the morning without having breakfast, then eat a big lunch, a big dinner, and then go to sleep, they may gain a lot of fat and their weight will increase. So, contrary to what you may think, you can gain weight by skipping a meal because you will end up eating more. Your body absorbs more calories in a state of starvation, so such an extreme diet plan may have the opposite effect and make you put on weight. Of course, it may also work to reduce your weight, so at the end of the day, it all depends on how well you can maintain your moderation.

The human body is made up of many different parts, such as nails, hair, skin, muscles, fat, nerve cells, and bones. To keep them nourished, you need to take in a certain amount of nutrition. So, I recommend that people who have tried these kinds of meal-cutting plans think about these points.

I changed my eating habits in my late 40s

For years, I hardly got sick and have lived a healthy life. Although it may not be good for a religious leader, it made me less sympathetic to sick people. But then, I experienced a serious illness in my late 40s, which is an age when people usually get ill. This experience led me to think deeply about health.

I had always been slightly chubby since I was young. I tried to lose weight several times, but it kept disrupting my work every time because I would easily get worn out and collapse. So, I always ended up having to prioritize work and keep my body weight without losing it. But I could not help but feel a little too heavy. I weighed too much because relative to how much I exercised, I was eating too many high-calorie foods.

After recovering from the serious illness, I realized that I needed to reduce my weight. I also realized that I was drinking too much liquids. So I began to strictly control my diet. To lose weight, I began by getting rid of excess water from my body. I incorporated more exercises that made me sweat a lot and also walked more, all while controlling the amount of liquid I took. To get slimmer, I adopted the two-meals-a-day diet and only had lunch and dinner. Doctors usually say that we should not skip breakfast, but I cut breakfast, had a light meal for lunch, usually noodles such as *somen* (Japanese thin wheat noodles), *soba* (buckwheat noodles), or pasta, and only ate an average amount for dinner. By doing this, I started losing about 2 kg (about five lb) every month. Of course, I was going for walks as well, but I learned from this experience that skipping breakfast will make you lose 2 kg a month.

After I lost about 10 kg (about 22 lb) through this two-meals-a-day diet, I went a little further to reach the standard body weight for my height. But then, I began losing hair. My hair is all natural now; I have not had a hair transplant and I do not wear a wig either. But after I lost 10 kg, I began losing my hair a lot in the shower and other places. I realized that I wasn't taking in enough nutrition for my hair, so I returned to having three meals a day, with a light breakfast. Then, I stopped losing weight. Until then, I kept dropping 2 kg, every month, but when that stopped, my hair also stopped falling out.

I have a lot of hair, so even when I wash it three times a day, I do not lose much or go bald. People often envy me for this. People are said to lose about a hundred strands every time they wash it, so you would think that washing it three times a day would make you bald in a year. Luckily, I have a lot of hair and I do not lose much. Anyhow, I learned from this experience that you will lose more hair if you cut down on its basic ingredients.

The problem with the drink-more-water diet and the low-sugar diet

Eating food with high sodium will make you drink more water, so your body will end up retaining more of it. Having excess fluid in you will make you more susceptible to various kinds of disease, especially ones related to your internal organs. So, you need to be careful about this as well, particularly if you drink a lot of water compared to others.

For a long time, books on dieting have often recommended drinking a lot of water as one of the methods for losing weight. They say that you should drink two liters of water every day, or drink a cup of water when you wake up in the morning. The purpose of this method is probably to make you feel full and not feel like eating by drinking a lot of water that has, of course, no calories. So, I do not necessarily think it is a good idea. Drinking a lot of water may be effective for people who can excrete it well or who run a lot. But I think the idea of getting healthier just by drinking a lot of water is a little questionable.

Another diet method that concerns me is the low-sugar diet, which is very popular now. I saw in a newspaper a large advertisement for a book with the slogan, "Once you are over 50, stop taking in sugar." But I am skeptical about this diet method, too. In my case, I do a lot of work that requires me to use my brain, such as reading books, writing books, and giving lectures. The main nutrient for the brain is sugar; glucose is its only energy source. In the same way that a car cannot run without gas, the brain cannot function without sugar. So, if you stop taking in sugar altogether, your body will have to use the glucose stored in your body.

If you have enough glucose in your body, it might be able to supplement it, but if it drops to a certain level, your body will suffer in the long run. The low-sugar diet has only begun recently, so you will see the effect of it within 10 to 20 years.

When people age, many of them suffer from dementia in their late years as a result of a decline in their brain function. They behave in unusual ways and sometimes cause trouble to those around them. I am afraid that cutting down on sugar may cause you to have similar problems in your later years. Of course, those who are overweight should refrain from taking in too much sugar, but cutting it out completely may not be such a good idea.

Buddhist monks are not strict vegetarians

The same is true with meat. Consuming too much of it can make you susceptible to various diseases, but I do

The Miracle Power to Overcome Illness

not think that cutting back on it completely is a good idea either. There are people who are strict vegetarians leading usual lives, so it is not impossible to live without it. However, in the modern age, people are brought up eating a balanced meal since childhood, so if they suddenly take up an extreme diet, they may fall ill.

Fasting has been a method of spiritual discipline since the old times, and vegetarianism is similar to this discipline. Based on a religious idea that says, "You must not take the lives of other living beings," some people adopt a vegetarian diet, believing that they should not eat meat because killing animals is a bad deed. Some religious groups uphold such a doctrine in their activities. So I do not mean to deny vegetarianism altogether.

If you actually saw an animal being slaughtered, you would certainly not feel like eating its meat. Since old times, there has been a precept in Buddhism that forbids people from eating the meat of an animal they saw being killed or that they heard was killed for them. However, although many people believe that Buddhist monks adhere to vegetarianism, they are not entirely vegetarians. In Shakyamuni Buddha's days, monks received alms from lay families who ate ordinary food, so they received all kinds of food in their bowls. They would eat everything that was put in their bowls, including meat, so they were not fully vegetarians. It is just that, in later generations, some monks felt pity for animals and had tofu and green onions to substitute meat. Many schools of Buddhism eventually followed suit.

One of the reasons these monks did not eat meat was that their standard of living was quite low. Another reason was to restrain their lust. By not eating high-calorie food, such as meat, they could "artificially" create a state of meditation or concentration. Or perhaps they were just taking a nap [*laugh*]; if you lack calories, you cannot be active. In that sense, taking in fewer calories enabled them to restrain their sexual desires. In modern days, however, not many people can adopt such a lifestyle. If you are working, I believe it is important to eat a decent amount of meals, exercise, and live a well-balanced life.

Not everyone can adopt a vegetarian diet

Some people tell others not to eat meat by emphasizing the fact that animals are being killed. The spirit of Mr. Masaharu Taniguchi, whom I mentioned earlier, said in his spiritual message that it is not good to eat meat. According to his ideas, when animals such as pigs, cows, or roosters are killed, they feel sad, and their sad emotion circulates their blood as poison. So, by eating their meat, you are taking in poison.

Mr. Taniguchi rarely put a portrait of himself in his books. He was a scrawny man of about 150 cm (5 ft) and often weighed less than 40 kg (90 lb). Maybe, he had a weak stomach. As he lived through World War II, he probably suffered from malnutrition. He had such physical conditions and that is why he advocated vegetarianism, meaning not everyone should follow his lifestyle.

In contrast, the late former Japanese prime minister Kakuei Tanaka often ate salty food, typical of the local food in his hometown, Niigata Prefecture. He liked to pour a lot of soy sauce over his richly-tasting *sukiyaki* (Japanese hot pot dish). Because of his high-sodium diet, he suffered from high blood pressure, which led to a stroke. This was quite predictable. So, we must prevent ourselves from contracting illnesses that are commonly caused by extreme diets.

The Mindset to Have During and After Recovering from an Illness

During the recovery period, train your body little by little

You need to pay good attention to your weight and fitness and prevent yourself from developing an illness. If you find that some parts of your body have weakened, train them little by little.

Whether or not you have strong legs and hips will make a big difference, especially when you become older. Elderly people are more prone to tripping and falling and that can lead them to breaking their bones. In most cases, if they are then bedridden for too long, they cannot make a full recovery. That is because their bodies weaken unless they use them.

When you fall ill or get injured, you may really have to be confined to bed for some time and be unable to do anything during that period. But once you are on your way to recovery, you should proactively train your body little by little and be strongly determined to get back on your feet. Your doctor may insist that you rest, but if you remain lying on your bed for too long, different parts of your body, such as your muscles and bones, will weaken and they may not restore their original strength. So, you need to summon up courage and make efforts to rebuild your body and regain your physical strength.

Doctors focus on the negatives

Doctors, in general, worry too much; not necessarily all, but many of them are like that. Why? Let me explain the reason. Medical schools are difficult to get into, so many people go to cram schools for years and take the entrance exam multiple times until they get accepted. At the cram schools, they are constantly "threatened" by their teachers who say, "You will not pass at this rate. You will fail again." So, many of them develop symptoms similar to obsessive-compulsive disorder.

Cram schools that specialize in preparing students for university entrance exams are a kind of "fear industry." The teachers often threaten their students by saying things like, "You will fail again," so inevitably, students will study harder even if it means sacrificing their sleep. As a result, they get used to a demerit system and tend to develop a strong fear of making mistakes. For this reason, I feel that a good percentage of doctors have "genes" that make them focus on finding faults.

They are overly concerned about the faults of things and focus on the negatives.

But doctors who focus on finding faults may actually be good doctors. Overly optimistic doctors who say things like, "Let it be and you'll be just fine" are, in a way, difficult to trust so I cannot make a general statement about it. However, if your doctor seems a little gloomy and has a strong tendency to focus on finding faults, you need to be careful not to be in complete tune with their negative views on life. Otherwise, you may be put under their "spell."

Furthermore, doctors just like to make statements such as, "There is an X percent chance that you will recover" or "You have about X years left to live" and just state the figures they studied and memorized. But I would like them to refrain from easily making such statements as they are not fortune tellers. People should not believe everything doctors say. Unless you have the will to go against what they tell you, you may really end up dying just as they say you would, so you must be careful.

Have the wish to be of help to God or Buddha and develop good lifestyle habits

If a doctor is putting such a "spell" on you, protect yourself by telling yourself, "I'm getting better and healthier, day by day."

Let me refer to ducks as an example. Ducks can float and swim in a pond, but if in a tub of water, you put a duck and pour detergent into it, the duck will immediately drown. This is because a duck's feathers are coated with oil, which repels water and prevents its feathers from getting wet. That is how it manages to float on water. So, the moment a laundry detergent is poured into the water, the duck will drown. It will sink and die.

Now, let's think of this in terms of humans. What would correspond to this oil that repels water and keeps the duck's feathers dry? That is the wish to improve yourself even a little and to be of help to God or Buddha. By firmly wishing for this and making constant efforts physically and mentally, you can create your own "oil" to "waterproof" yourself, much like the oil that keeps a duck from drowning. So it is important to have good thought habits that come from faith.

Try to accept the Will of God or Buddha, even if your illness is not cured

Illnesses can be healed through religious faith, but in terms of probability, you cannot say that they will be cured 100 percent of the time. There are many cases where illnesses are not cured. Even if you take a *kigan* (ritual prayer) or recite prayers to recover from illness at a Happy Science *shoja* (temple or monastery), there are times when your illness may not get better. When that happens and the priest who conducted the kigan ceremony becomes very disappointed and loses confidence, the ritual prayers he or she conducts will truly become less effective. The same is true for a person who is taking a kigan to cure illnesses. Sometimes, it can become ineffective if they remember and think too much about a person who still died after taking the same kigan in the past. So ultimately, what is important is to entrust everything to God or Buddha and continue doing what you must do.

In times of illness, look back on your life afresh

While I should not talk much about the benefits of illness, as I said earlier, illness is a good time for you to look back on your life afresh. It is a chance for you to reflect on how you have been living so far.

Most people who fall ill in their 40s have overworked themselves. They have pushed themselves too far. Usually, those who were athletic during their school days are confident about their health. But if they do not take good care of their bodies for over 20 years, and instead frequently go for drinks after work, consume too many calories, and are always sleep deprived, they may well fall ill in their 40s. This is quite common. On the other hand, some people will suddenly look aged after retirement; their bodies weaken and do not function properly. To avoid these situations, you should carefully look at yourself objectively. When you fall ill, you need to once again examine your lifestyle habits, thinking habits, and work habits.

People who fall ill usually overdo things. For example, they overwork themselves or work long hours, drink too much by saying they have a high alcohol tolerance, smoke too much by saying they can smoke 40 cigarettes a day, or pull all-nighters for three consecutive days and boast about it. These people will, at some point in life, suddenly fall ill. But according to the law of cause and effect, this is a natural consequence. They are usually the type of people who do not listen to others' advice, so they must control their behaviors themselves. If you are married and have a good partner who cares about your health, you should listen well to his or her advice. You must listen well to the advice of those who care about you.

The Spiritual Influences behind Illness

The spirit of a living person can sometimes cause an illness

People who are robust tend to think that they can get everything done with their minds alone. Their aggressive nature is apt to make them a conceited person like a *tengu* (long-nosed goblin). At work, they would instantly belittle their coworkers who are incompetent thinking, "I alone am the honored one" and are self-righteous. With such a mentality, they are likely to push through and climb up the corporate ladder. But they are usually disliked by many people or are the target of other people's resentful thought energy.

During the Heian Period (9th-12th century), it was commonly believed that people can be cursed by the dead, or be visited by *ikiryo* (spirit of a living person). Although most people today do not believe in these things, they still exist in reality. In the beginning, I used to help and persuade the spirits of the dead, who were disturbing me, into going back to heaven. But once Happy Science was firmly established, these spirits no longer came to me but I was instead confronted by ikiryo, or the strong thought energies of living people.

People who are full of dissatisfaction, grumbles, complaints, and anger emit strong negative thought energies, and these thought energies manifest as ikiryo. These ikiryo will then come to me. Ikiryo seems to be a guardian spirit of the living that carries his or her strong thoughts. If you are constantly affected by such negative thought energies, you are more likely to get ill. So, people in the Heian Period were not necessarily wrong.

Sometimes, a person's thoughts can become so strong that their ikiryo constantly comes to you. When this happens, you will get a clear vision of their face, even if they may live far away. So it is important to take measures against ikiryo, or the strong thoughts of living people. To prevent them from coming to you, you need to be careful not to do things that might invite strong grudges from others. If you have some unresolved problems in your relationships, try to make amendments to improve the relationships. But if you cannot do that because things have turned so sour that neither of you wants to see the other, try reflecting on yourself and look for any mistakes on your part. Then, apologize to them in your heart and adopt the heart to congratulate them. In this way, you can fight off illnesses caused by ikiryo.

In other words, ikiryo can send you the thought energy of illness, or a kind of curse, which will make you feel unwell. For example, it has been said from old times that a woman who is involved in a love triangle is likely to contract gynecological diseases. This happens

The Miracle Power to Overcome Illness

partly because of negative spiritual influences. When your mind is not "round" but has "dents" or a "jagged surface," ikiryo will use their "ice ax" to hook on to those rough points and sneak into your mind. Therefore, you should polish your mind well so that it emits light, and strive to stay away from any negative spiritual influences.

You can expel possessing spirits through religious belief and the power of light

Not only will you be affected by the negative thought energy of living people, but you can also be possessed by an evil spirit that has similar vibrations to that thought energy. In this world, many people die of illness and some of them cannot return to heaven and instead become lost spirits. These spirits wander around their houses, workplaces, or hospitals, and of course, you can also find them in graveyards. If you happen to develop some connection to these spirits, you can get possessed by them.

Therefore, when you go to a hospital, you will not only receive medical treatment but you can also become possessed by one of these lost spirits. Many people die in hospitals, and those among them who have nowhere else to go after death will remain there as spirits. If both the patients and doctors are materialists, the patients who died cannot understand why they are still "alive." They will have no clue of what is going on. Since doctors are not monks, they cannot teach them about the world after death. That is why these spirits have no choice but to wander around the hospitals. And when they happen to see a patient with the same illness and similar symptoms being hospitalized in the room they were in, they would instantly go into them and possess them. Things like this can happen. We sometimes see cases in which patients suddenly say things that they would never usually say or patients whose personalities suddenly change. This is usually because they are possessed.

This is generally how spiritual possession happens, and these possessing spirits can be expelled through religious belief and the power of light. To do this, first, you need to study the Truth. Calm your mind and make it as smooth as the surface of a still lake. Concentrate your mind so that you are on a different wavelength from evil thoughts. Also, try not to grumble and complain like how people who are ill commonly do. If you happen to be jealous of healthy and successful people, make an effort to congratulate them.

People who are ill are apt to be frustrated and discontented. They tend to complain a lot and sometimes vent their frustration on their family. They are often very angry as well. However, in times of illness, people should try to be grateful for the life they were given in this world and for having been allowed to live up until this day. They should especially give gratitude to those who nurtured them in their childhood, even if those people are no longer around, as well as their parents who raised them to adulthood. They should also try to remember the people who supported them, including those who have already passed away, and send out thoughts of gratitude to those people, too.

In addition, try to find joy in small, insignificant things. Only when you are hospitalized can you notice the pretty little flowers in a vase placed in your room. Try to find small things like this, which you usually overlooked when you were healthy. When people visit you at the hospital, you should try to find and appreciate the good points or beautiful qualities in them that you may have neglected to this day.

People who commit suicide to escape from illness cannot easily return to heaven

Illness can often become the reason for families to fall apart. For example, let's take a family who is already struggling to balance and maintain both work and family life. If one person were to fall ill, other family members would lose a considerable amount of time and energy in taking care of the sick person, and there would also be unexpected expenses. If the parents still need money for their children's education, for example, they could be placed in an extremely difficult situation. They will need a great deal of mental power to overcome this problem.

Sometimes, a sick person may choose to commit suicide. Upon finding that their illness is incurable and that they have to live with it for the rest of their life, these people may commit suicide thinking that they will only be a burden to their family by causing them financial difficulties. For this reason, some may jump out of a window or from the rooftop of a hospital. But in most cases, people who die in this way cannot return to heaven. Some of them commit suicide from a materialistic standpoint. Others may not be materialists but still commit suicide without hesitation because they believe in the eternity of the soul. However, people who escape their lives for this reason cannot easily return to heaven.

The spirits of these people can neither go to heaven nor hell. Many of them become earth-bound spirits, wander around the hospital, and accumulate evil deeds by possessing the patients at the hospital and making them suffer. In other cases, those spirits fall to a world of hell for those who have committed suicide. There, the spirits continue to kill themselves again and again. Because they do not understand the meaning of death, they repeatedly commit suicide, thinking that they are not dead yet. This is frightening but a reality.

Spirits can possess people based on the Law of the Same Wavelengths

The spirits of people who have committed suicide sometimes remain in this world. In places where such spirits are, other people also commit suicide in a similar way one after another. For instance, there are houses and schools that have become a suicide spot for people. We can assume that those who have the habit of wrist-cutting are possessed by evil spirits, so usually, in this case, evil spirits have possessed their family.

The Miracle Power to Overcome Illness

The first thing these people need to consider is whether there is anyone in their families or relatives who is likely to have become lost spirits after death. Or, a spirit unrelated to your family can possess your family member if his or her thoughts are attuned to that spirit, based on the Law of the Same Wavelengths. This is the same as how a TV monitor displays an image when it is tuned to a particular channel.

A while ago, there was a movie about a cursed videotape, where a ghost would appear after someone watches it, although nowadays, we use DVDs, not videotapes. This was what happened in the movie. But in a spiritual sense, similar kinds of things can happen in real life. Spirits can come to you through some kind of connection, be it a videotape, DVD, cell phone, or any other electronic device. If your wavelength is attuned to those of the evil spirits, they can appear before you.

In my case, this happens even through newspapers. When there is an article about someone's passing on the front page, it is troublesome for me. When I see his or her picture and worry that their spirit might come, in many cases, they visit me in a few seconds, or ten seconds at the most. But not all the spirits can come to me even though I see their pictures. That is usually because they do not have a close tie with me, or they are still not aware that they are dead. Otherwise, spirits who have their photos printed in newspapers will often visit me.

I used to be very troubled by these visits, so my secretaries who were on the early shift would wake up at five o'clock in the morning, check all the newspapers between five and six o'clock, and stick a piece of white paper over the photo of any deceased people so that I did not have to look at it. Nowadays, they no longer do this, maybe to save time and effort.

Sometimes, the spirit of a famous person who died will support us by giving us a spiritual message. Some famous people would even give us spiritual messages even when we did not ask them to, but those cannot be helped. There is a term, "celebrity tax" in Japan; conducting the spiritual messages of famous people who died, in other words, showing their "resurrection," may help to awaken many people. So I record their spiritual messages because I feel I should benefit the world.

"The True Words Spoken By Buddha" is effective in expelling evil spirits

Earlier, I cited the example of how duck feathers are coated with oil to repel water. In terms of spiritual possession, the same can be said here. Just as I mentioned in the example of the movie about a cursed video, you can easily be connected to evil spirits if your wavelengths are attuned to theirs. So, you need to find ways to avoid connecting to them.

If you are already possessed by evil spirits, the most effective way to expel them is to use the Happy Science sutra, "The True Words Spoken By Buddha." You can recite it yourself or have someone else recite it for you. The CD of my reciting the Happy Science basic sutras, which is 30 minutes long, is also available. As far as I have experienced, very few evil spirits can keep possessing a person after playing the entire CD. I am sure that most evil spirits will leave you by then.

The fundamental solution
is to have a positive mindset

If your mind is attracting evil spirits like a magnet, they will come back to you again and again, no matter how many times you expel them. In this case, just listening to my CD alone will not be a complete solution. If it is your mind that is inviting evil spirits, then you need to stop doing so. In order to do that, you must learn the Truth, practice self-reflection, and pray so that your wavelengths are different from those of the evil spirits. You should have a positive mindset and strive to look at the bright side of things as you study the Truth.

It is very hard for sick people to have a positive mindset. Almost always, they are drawn to the negative side of things. So, if you are ill, try to make an effort to look at the positive side of things, little by little. It is also important that you try to put on a smile. Sometimes, your doctor may tell you various negative things about what may happen to you in the future, but you should think that you could be an exception and hope that you will get better soon, even a little. You must keep believing strongly that you will get better. Also, having someone with a positive mindset around you can be of great help. You should be thankful if you have one.

Miracles hardly occur in hospitals with strong materialistic vibrations

Miracles rarely happen in hospitals because many people there have strong materialistic vibrations. Hospitals are filled with negative thought energies. People there believe, "There is no way illnesses can be cured through prayer or some kind of psychic power." So, it is extremely hard to cure illnesses through miracles in hospitals.

Some doctors understand the Truth and accept the possibility of miracles, but this depends on the person. Usually, doctors who only use the knowledge they gained at medical school to treat people will consider medical treatment as a mere procedure. They think that treating illness is the same as repairing a car. They believe that, once a body part is "broken," the only way to repair is to replace it. Most doctors think like this. Miracles hardly occur around such people, who have strong materialistic thought energies.

There are, of course, other types of doctors. Some are broad-minded. They can see that patients have different mindsets, so they avoid making decisions based only on statistics. They may say, for example, "This patient seems to have a strong mentality, so perhaps he can be cured." What is more, virtuous doctors may even admit there are exceptional cases and say, "This patient's illness might unexpectedly turn for the better." You are lucky if you are blessed with such a doctor.

The Tendency of the Body and Mind Can Be the Cause of Your Illnesses

If you have an extreme lifestyle, try to fix it to a normal level

At some point in life, most people go through illness. Sometimes, your illness can be caused by the tendency of your body and mind that you have developed since childhood. So, I advise you to put enough effort into preventing illnesses through it.

Your tendency can also play a big role when you are recovering, undergoing rehabilitation, or replanning how you will live from now on. If you have any habits or mental tendencies that are extreme or unusual in the eyes of others, try to amend them and live a healthier lifestyle.

Maybe you have certain habits that you struggle to resist doing. For example, you could have a bad drinking habit and you cannot go without drinking a certain amount of alcohol. Or perhaps you have a bad smoking habit where you smoke dozens of cigarettes every day. If so, you could make an effort to reduce the amount you consume. That is one way to fix your bad tendency.

The same is true with people who tend to overwork and are always exhausted. Highly competent people, in particular, tend to do everything themselves. These people need to learn to receive help and support from others. They should be modest and think about how to ask for help from others.

If you study management, you will learn that management is not about achieving something on your own but it is a method to achieve something greater with the help of many people. But this is easier said than done. Especially, the founders of small and medium-sized companies tend to believe that things do not go well unless they do the work themselves. They can hardly entrust their work to others and that is why they try to do everything themselves. Unfortunately, these people will become overworked at some point.

This may be when their company grows too big for them to handle or when they suffer from difficult times of being in debt. Or it may be when they face an economic downturn or experience discord in their families. Various challenges will arise when running a company. At such times, return to the basics of management and reconsider your work style. Is there really nothing you can entrust to others? Check and see if you are not being stubborn and just sticking to your own ways. Or, maybe, you are having trouble delegating your work because you cannot explain how it is done to others. Please consider these points well.

Establish procedures for your work
and delegate it to others

Those who cannot entrust their work to others are most probably doing much of their work through their intuition. So they cannot clearly explain how to do their work to others. This is especially the case for those with craftsmanship. Because they cannot teach their skills to others, they just say, "Watch and learn." Even today, chefs often say things like, "I cannot teach you knife skills, so watch and learn," or "It is impossible to teach how to make broth or soup, so just 'steal' the recipe from other chefs through tasting."

I once read a book written by a chef who worked at a restaurant in the Imperial Hotel in Japan. In the book, he said that, since his senior chefs did not teach him how to make the restaurant's best broth, he studied it by tasting the soup leftovers before washing the pots. Then, at night, or when he was not busy, he would experiment and explore the ratio of each ingredient

The Miracle Power to Overcome Illness

that was used to make the broth. So, he learned on his own by "stealing" from senior chefs.

Competent people often find other people's work inferior and believe that no one else can do their work. Even so, they need to make an effort to delegate their work to others and reduce their burden a little. Otherwise, their companies will not grow further and develop as a whole. They must know this.

These people are working hard, but they haven't got a clue as to what kind of work they are actually doing. So at some point, they need to make time and sort out their work. They need to organize the work procedures they usually follow or the way they make judgments. You can start with something simple. Make a note or jot it down on a piece of paper. Write down the procedures and the methods you take and organize them, little by little. This will also help you organize your thoughts.

If you cannot teach others how you do your work, you will often become hard on them and end up doing it all by yourself. As a result, you will push yourself too much and often end up falling ill. So if you aim to make further progress, establish the procedures for your work and delegate it to others. By doing so, you can create "free time" for yourself to move on to the next step and take up a new project. In this way, your business will develop as a whole.

Do not hoard your work

Some people hoard work to themselves and do not teach others how to do it so others cannot take their jobs. This is how public servants usually work. They basically work in this way.

This is what I learned in the early days of my political science class at university. The professor teaching the class said, "Many of you will probably become public servants after graduation. Once you become one, you need to make sure that you become an indispensable figure at work. You are at great risk if other people can take your place and do your work when you are not around. You need to set your work in a way that your colleagues will have a hard time handling your work on your days off. Then, you will be regarded as important and indispensable, allowing you to keep working for a long time and climb the ladder of success. You will not be promoted if others can also do your work and can replace you at any time." I learned this in the early days of my political science class.

This attitude actually goes against the ideas taught in business management. But in public offices, you are in "danger" if you can easily be replaced by someone else. If you are easily replaceable and are to be hospitalized, for example, your colleagues would tell you, "Oh, you are in a hospital. Take as much time as you need to recover. You can be hospitalized for a year or even three years and we won't have any problems. Anyone can replace you and do your work, so don't worry." This is why public servants tend to create complicated work procedures so that no one else but they can do the job. They always guard some part of their work so that others will not be able to proceed without them. In this way, they maintain their authority. That is how they usually work. The same is true with chefs. They always try to hoard the secret recipe to themselves. This is how things are in some occupations.

However, if you want to develop your business based on business management, you should establish the work procedures of the standard and common tasks, and delegate them to others. Unless you take this approach, you will not be able to develop your business further.

In general, public offices do not make profits, even though the number of their workers is increasing. But private business companies must think carefully about how they carry out their work. I, too, am thinking about this. I try to delegate work when I can, and I make an effort to simplify my work. Even so, more and more work comes up, so it is not so easy.

The Miracle Power to Overcome Illness

To prevent yourself from getting ill, you must remember that there are situations when you need to ask others for help. You also need to listen to the advice of other people who warn you or stop you when you are pushing yourself too much. There are also times when you need to control your ego. Please keep these things in mind.

Overcome Your Illness
with Miracle Power

Prayer can help increase the chance of recovery

I talked about the importance of making efforts to change the state of your mind by practicing self-reflection and studying the Truth. In addition to these, the power of prayer is also effective. Praying may not be suited for Japanese people, but it is common in other countries.

There is research overseas that acknowledges that prayers are effective to a certain degree. Researchers compared the progress of illness between two groups of patients, where one group received no prayers and another group received prayers from their church friends. According to the research paper I read, although the power of prayer did not have a drastic effect, it raised the chance of recovery by about five percent. By studying the two groups of patients and looking at the data, it was observed that there were higher chances for the patients who received prayers from other people to recover. When many people prayed for the sick people and the sick people also knew about it, the probability increased by several percent.

From this, we can see that in times of illness, you are likely to recover when you feel that other people need you or want you to get better. Such positive feelings from others will help you rid of your negative thought energy, as well as repel spiritual beings that you are attracting with your negativity. In this sense, prayer can be effective.

Of course, supernatural phenomena, or miracles, do not occur often. Speaking of miracles, the Bible describes the miracles of Jesus. For example, when Jesus put some mud that was mixed with his saliva on a blind man's eye, who had been blind since birth, he became able to see.

There is another story of a miracle that happened to a man named Lazarus, who had been dead for four days and was put in a tomb. When Jesus said, "Lazarus is not dead but has fallen asleep. Lazarus, come out!" Lazarus came out of the tomb with strips of linen wrapped around him. This is quite scary when you think about it. A dead body with most probably a foul stench came back to life like a zombie. Legends of zombies have a long history in the Christian culture; there are many stories about zombies and Dracula. Anyhow, such a miracle really occurred. But the fact that Lazarus' story has been handed down for 2,000 years shows how rare such a case is. Even so, things like this do happen in reality.

The miracle of Lourdes that happened
before the eyes of a scientist

There are also stories about Hansen's disease being cured in the Bible. Many such miracles have occurred in later generations as well, but the chances of miracles happening are actually very small.

For example, there are stories about the miracles of Lourdes. According to these stories, illnesses are cured when people go on a pilgrimage to the spring of Lourdes in southern France. Nearly one million people make a pilgrimage there every year, but ever since it began more than 100 years ago, only less than a hundred cases of miracles have been officially approved by the Vatican. Compared to the number of people making the pilgrimage, the number of "official" miracles is very small. So in terms of probability, the chances of miracles occurring are extremely low. This probability is not so different from the number of hospitalized patients who have unexpectedly recovered from illnesses.

Regardless, the power of faith can sometimes cure an illness. When Alexis Carrel, who later won the Nobel Prize in Physiology or Medicine, accompanied his patients to Lourdes, he witnessed a miracle. Right before his very eyes, he saw a woman become cured from a heavy physical ailment she was suffering from in just a few hours after bathing in the spring. She no longer needed a wheelchair or a walking stick. Such a case has been reported.

It is hard for me to think he was lying, so this miracle must be a true story. I believe heaven's will was at work. I believe that the spirits of the heavenly world had him witness the miracle so that the story would spread to many people. Miracles happen from time to time because, without it, people are likely to lose faith. Miracles can happen to someone who has faith or when there is a witness who will spread the story and guide many people.

The miracle power of Happy Science
will get stronger as it grows

Many people at local branches and shojas of Happy Science have also experienced miracles of their incurable disease getting cured. The general public has little interest in such stories because they are happening in religion, but if these things happened in hospitals, they would become big news.

A multitude of unbelievable miracles are indeed occurring. At one time, when I visited a local branch and walked through the aisle between the audience to get to the lecture podium, one lady in the audience was cured of her illness. She came to my lecture on crutches, but no longer needed them after the lecture. Doctors would lose their minds if they heard such a story. In Christian churches, sometimes illnesses are cured through the laying of hands, where a priest places one or both hands on a person's head. But I did not even need to touch the person; I just walked by the person, and her illness was cured. There have also been cases where our members have been cured of their illnesses just by watching Happy Science movies. Recently, I even heard that someone was cured of their illness just by receiving a Happy Science flyer on the street.

As Happy Science grows larger, our power will get stronger, and the miracle power of many of our believers will also increase. So, I think more illnesses will be cured. As our group continues to develop, more miracles will occur at an important time and an important place (some of the miracles that happened to Happy Science members are included at the end of this book).

What I want to ask of you is the following. If you can, please practice self-reflection and meditation, and pray. In your day-to-day life, if you have a "stock" of gratitude and kindness that you were meant to give to others, please be more explicit and express it to them. But before anything, be grateful that you were born into this world, that you have been given life to this day, and that you are still living thanks to the support of many people. This heart of gratitude will let the light of heaven reach you.

Sometimes, I need to give a talk on illnesses, too. So today, I gave an overview of illness with the title, "The Miracle Power to Overcome Illnesses."

CHAPTER

2

Question and Answer
Sessions on Illnesses

Q1

How to Overcome
Eldercare Problem in the Family

QUESTIONER A

Today, we are seeing more and more cases of people having to take care of their family members who are ill or suffering from dementia. For this reason, many people are put in difficult situations where they have to make a decision such as to quit their jobs to take care of their family or put the elderly in care homes. I would like you to give us some advice on how to overcome the eldercare problem in the family.

Increased life expectancy has called for
long-term eldercare

RYUHO OKAWA

In a way, no one saw this coming. The reason people are now living longer is due to the large investments made into the medical field and having many smart people study medicine and do research. For a long time, the average human life expectancy was said to be around 50 years, but now it has gone up to 80 and 90 years for Japanese people. As a result, the length of time that elderlies require care from others has also increased. If around the age of 50 was the average life expectancy, then even if people require eldercare, it would only be for a short amount of time. Or if anything, unless an accident of some sort makes them call for such care, they may not even need it.

Life expectancy has certainly increased and this shows that advancement in medical science has had some effects on prolonging life. But, of course, medical science may not be the only contributing factor. There are also other factors including improved food supply and a more affluent society. So, the improvements in the food supply and the economy, as well as the advancement of medicine, have all contributed to extending the human lifespan. But what people could not see coming as a result of it is the demand for eldercare. This is one of the major reasons for the problems that are arising now. In other words, the government only focused on extending our lifespan through medical procedures and did not strategize any plans for how to deal with eldercare and the financial burden that comes with it. Neither did each family household imagine that an eldercare issue would arise in their family.

Support from the government and local offices will hit its limit

Humans have long believed that eternal youth and longevity are the source of happiness. We can see this in ancient Chinese stories, too.

But just like how things are now, if longevity gives rise to the need for people to be nursed in their later years, young individuals who are fit to work in the family will need to take on the role of a carer. For instance, if a mother or wife is the carer, she will not be able to do other work, and in some cases, her children may need to quit their jobs to help her. It costs a lot of money to hire professional caregivers. So, if it exceeds the family's earnings, they will not be able to afford it. That is why people turn to the government and local offices for support, but the government and local offices themselves are suffering from budget deficits and are about to hit their limit. Meaning, the system on the whole is not functioning.

If life goes well, humans are biologically said to live up to 120 years old, but people usually die before then for various reasons including illness. Humans have been pursuing eternal youth and longevity, believing that longevity is the condition to live happily. But as life expectancy increased, the need for eldercare created a shadow on people's lives.

The suicide rate may rise among the elderly

What we need to be wary of from now on is the potential situation where the elderly are abandoned by their family, much like the story of the Japanese folk tale, *Ubasute Yama* (literally, "Mountain Where Old Women Were Abandoned"). We must also be wary of elderly abuse. Moreover, we may see a rise in the suicide rates of elderly people who are receiving care.

These elderly people are not necessarily committing suicide because their minds are full of negative thoughts.

I have heard that, nowadays, more and more elderly people are committing suicide because they do not want to be a burden on their families or cause them financial trouble. But honestly speaking, taking care of an elderly person who suffers from dementia and has been bedridden for over 10 years is a heavy burden, so their families will reach a limit one day. This is a difficult issue. In short, we have gained something by extending our lives, so now we have to sacrifice something for what we have gained. This is what we are facing. Having said that, as more problems regarding eldercare surface and become a social problem, more people will start thinking about how to deal with it. This may help us find a solution.

The spirit of independence as seen
in the life of Seiroku Honda

People who would already be dead under the standards of older times are now living longer. Therefore, if you wish to live longer, you must also wish to live out your life in good health. It is important that you aim to "live well and die well" and stay fit until the last day of your life.

Back in the day, I used to read a lot of books by Seiroku Honda*, who worked like a superhuman. He mostly lived before World War II, and despite living in such times, traveled abroad as many as 19 times and wrote about 370 books. When he was young, he developed a habit of writing one page a day, which later became three pages a day, and before he knew it, he ended up writing more than 370 books. In his later years, he secluded himself in Ito City in the Izu Peninsula, where he led a self-sufficient life. Before that, he engaged

---

*Seiroku Honda (1866 – 1952) was a Japanese forestry scholar. He studied forestry in Germany and later became a professor at Tokyo Imperial University. He also designed many parks, including Hibiya Park.

in forestry and also amassed a huge fortune by investing in land and stocks. His name was even listed among Japan's richest people.

In Ito City, he lived like a hermit. Yet, he maintained a sharp mind to even write books about his life before passing away at age 85. Even in his twilight years, he would go out on a walk for 8 km (about 5 miles) every day after dinner to help with digestion. At the time, he also carried around a planner book with his name, address, and a message on it that said, "Should anything happen to me, please call my family. We will pay you back for any cost that has incurred." He must have been a superhuman to walk 8 km every night. It is even tough to walk that much during the daytime. He continued to write books and was active until his last moment came. This is an admirable way to end your life.

So, what this shows is that your mentality, more or less, plays an important role. In other words, even after you retire, you should train your body and mind, as well as explore the right eating habits. You must try to be independent and think, "I will continue to be able to do things for myself." If you can hold on to such thoughts for 10 or 20 years and continue to make efforts, things will gradually turn out that way. These are important points that each person should be mindful of.

People can become bedridden due to "love deficiency syndrome"

On the other hand, if you have an elderly person in your family, you need to know that they can sometimes become bedridden or cause a heavy burden to you and your family because they want to feel loved. This is also true in the field of psychology. These people want to be cared for and are desperate to get love from others, and that is why they end up needing the care of others. They are suffering from "love deficiency syndrome," meaning they are lacking a "mineral" called love.

To people who have become like this due to old age or other reasons, what you must do is to let them know, from time to time, how grateful you are for the things they have done for you and how you appreciate them. This is just like giving nutrients to plants. This effort will surely give them energy.

Build good relationships and help each other

In our final days, we all need to mutually help each other, so it is important to make efforts to build good relationships with others while we are young. This includes family members. It is not easy for a family who has been out of touch for years to build a close tie and a warm relationship with each other just because one of them got sick. You cannot suddenly form a close relationship with them that can last for 10 to 20 years. That is why you must think ahead and make efforts to accumulate good deeds and build good relationships with the people around you from a young age.

You never know who and when someone among your family members will fall ill and need help. So, as a form of "insurance," you need to think about nurturing someone within your family who can afford to take care of the sick. In other words, you must not only rely on external resources, such as support from the government and the local offices, or the money from life and health insurance. This does not necessarily have to be your own children; it can be your nephew or niece. Or, it could be someone you know from your workplace. This is why it is important to help others when you have the time or money. These people may well come to help you in times of need.

The late Japanese scholar and critic Shoichi Watanabe once said, "There are many troubles surrounding insurance and pension today. But although those who lived before World War II did not have any of those things, they still lived through their old age without any trouble." The reason behind this is that, back then, taking care of the elderly was the family's job. For generations, the younger family members had taken care of the elderly within the family. This was possible because it used to be a common duty. But nowadays, nuclear families are more common and individualism is on the rise. As society heads in this direction, people are increasingly dependent on, and seek aid from, the government and the local offices. This is, in fact, the current trend. But if the public support reaches its limit, there will be repercussions.

On the news, we hear many unpleasant terms like "lonely death" and "elderly bankruptcy," but I think they are actually serving as a kind of warning toward the modern trend. Everyone will eventually have to think about preparing themselves for their later years. Therefore, it is important that you build strong family bonds. You should also develop a network with your local community and nurture a spirit of mutual support.

Now is your chance to do so. This is one of the chances to change how things work. I believe religion can also play a big role in creating this strong network.

Develop a more religious mindset and interact with people face-to-face

It is said that about one-fourth of Japan's population is now aged over 65, and this will increase even more. Hospitals can only care for people until they die, but religion will continue to care for people even after death. So, it is important to build close relationships with others within your religious circle. When you are delivering Happy Science monthly magazines, for example, you should also try to talk with other members and build good relationships with them. In times of emergency, people outside of your family can sometimes be of help. I think there needs to be more mutual support among members of local communities.

Right now, things seem to be fine because the government and the local offices still can support the elderly despite a budget deficit. But the time will eventually come when the aged population becomes the majority and the public sector will no longer be able to support them. Even so, it is wrong to tell the elderly not to live long and to die sooner. So we need to create a society where people help each other more. Although religious groups in Japan are losing power, I believe that people need to work on developing a religious mindset and place more value on interacting with people face-to-face. In society, information is often conveyed one-sidedly, but we should rather create a society where there is more face-to-face interaction. We need to make these kinds of efforts to deal with an aging society.

To do this, although it may be tough in terms of management, I hope to create Happy Science local temples in every town so that our members can come together and help each other. In this way, there will always be someone available to help another in need.

We need to work together and help each other instead of relying too much on the public system.

Relying solely on caregivers
is a communist-like mindset

The idea of simply providing a caregiver to families in need is a communist-like mindset. Communist governments basically encourage both husband and wife to work. While couples are encouraged to have children, children are regarded as national assets. Communists believe that both parents should keep working while the government takes care of the children. Therefore, children are regarded as national property in communist countries. The idea that is currently prevailing in Japan is a little similar to this. However, unless children receive sufficient love and care from their parents, they will not want to take care of their parents. Only when children can acknowledge how much trouble they have caused their parents and how much their parents cared for them, will they look after their parents when they grow older.

Successful people should have the spirit of chivalry

It is difficult for every member of a family to become successful, but if you aspire to produce at least one successful person in your family, things will turn out that way. This can also be a member of your relatives like nephews and nieces. Family members and relatives should encourage each other to nurture at least one person who will go on to become successful. They should come together to support the one who has the potential. Then, in case of emergencies, the person who becomes successful will become like insurance for the family and will be able to support the rest of the family.

In life, someone in the family can get injured, ill, or die. But on the contrary, there will also be someone successful in the family. So do not be too affected by the negative factors. Instead, encourage those who are successful to be even more successful.

Recently, I saw a talk between the 14th Dalai Lama, who lives in exile, and Lady Gaga on a TV program. I am not sure if the Dalai Lama was joking or not, but he said to Lady Gaga something along the lines of, "Since you are good at making money, you should go ahead and make a lot more. People who are talented in making money should earn a lot and distribute it to those in need." He told her of the spirit of chivalry, which I often mention. He said something like, "You should make a lot of money. Do not think making money is wrong. Earn a lot and use it a lot." I found that he thinks quite flexibly.

Indeed, moneymaking requires talent. Some people are good at it, while others are not. Those without this talent will fail no matter what. So, people who are good at making money should go ahead and do so. And what is important is that these people then live by the spirit of chivalry.

Joint responsibility can mean
nobody's responsibility

First, you should aim to make someone in your family successful. If that does not work, widen your scope and aim to make one of your relatives successful. It is important that you have such an incentive. If both options do not work, expand your view even further and think in terms of community. As I said earlier, form a connection with people in your community who have the same religious faith, and help each other because you never know who will be the next in need. You should also help each other in times of disaster. In the same way, make an effort to lend a helping hand to any lonely elderly who are in need. It is important to give a part of the virtue you have accumulated to others.

Back in the day before World War II, it was often the case that the successful one supported the rest of their family. Since many families could not afford to educate all their children, they sent at least one child with potential to university. The child would then complete his studies at university while working, and upon graduation, other siblings would come to the city and live with him. The siblings would then find jobs or go to school while receiving support from the one who went first. In this way, if you do not have enough money to invest in every member of your family, then someone with a sense of mission should rise up to support the whole family. We need to create such a culture.

Ever since the Japanese civil law was amended after World War II, the traditional family system has been "dismantled" considerably. The current system (as opposed to the prewar system, where the eldest son succeeded the head of the family) encourages all the family members to take responsibility. However, joint responsibility can mean nobody's responsibility. Although everyone is encouraged to take responsibility, they will all try to avoid it. From the perspective of equality, parents must not treat their children unequally. However, for parents to raise a child who will be willing to take care of them when they get older, they will need to spend a good amount of time, energy, and money on him. I believe one way of solving this problem is to create a culture that encourages children to take care of their parents and pass this down to future generations.

Should the current trend continue and children refuse to take care of their parents, the civil law will need to be amended again. Instead of leaving everything to the nation, it is important that families and relatives consider taking care of each other. But in the end, I want to consider it as the mission of religion to take care of this issue.

I think the time will come when the current system will fall apart. Currently, the mass media is reporting how the government and local offices should take care of the elderly and create new systems. They are insisting on raising caregivers' salaries so that more people will apply for the job. But this will surely have negative effects on other areas. What they are saying will not be the fundamental solution to the problem.

Have the "It's enough" mind and practice the "Three Happinesses"

Another important point is to have the "It's enough" mind. Not everyone lives their life in affluence, like royalty or noble families. Some people do, but that is rare. So, you must learn to be content. Once you are earning enough money to lead a stable life, you need to reexamine your lifestyle, lead a simple life, and try to increase your savings. You should explore ways to get by even after dropping the level of your living standard.

In this sense, the idea of "Happiness Saving" is essential. Try not to use all of your money but save some. When you earn a lot of money or get a promotion, make sure that you do not use all that you earn. "Happiness Sharing" is another important idea. When you become economically successful or your business goes well, you should be willing to share your happiness with others. Moreover, the idea of "Happiness Planting," or planting fortune for the future, is also important.

The example of my aunt practicing
Happiness Planting

When I was an elementary school student, my novelist aunt, who was single, would come to my house on occasions like the New Year and summer holidays. She would give me some pocket money, sometimes ¥5,000 (US$33), and at other times, ¥10,000 (US$66). I was very happy about this as a child because children rarely got extra allowance. My parents would only give me ¥20 a day, which allowed me to only buy one candy. But when my aunt came to my house, she would give me ¥1,000 and then gave even more as I got older; it went from ¥1,000 to ¥5,000 and then to ¥10,000. What she was doing was "Happiness Planting." She was planting a fortune for her future. She probably thought that if her nephew became successful, she could rely on him if there was an emergency.

My aunt lived alone and continued to write novels even in her later years. When she was over 70, she lived in an apartment in which her friend also lived.

Apparently, she and her friend made a promise that if one of them fell ill, the other one would help. In her last days, she was hospitalized in Tokushima City but she continued to write her novels even as she lay in bed. *Tokushima Shimbun Newspaper* reported about this as a moving story, saying, "The novelist devoted her life to writing to the very end of her life."

While it was true that she devoted her life to writing, I, too, have "devoted myself" to my family. I sent the money I earned to my parents who lived in Shikoku. They then supported my aunt with that money by hiring a caregiver or visiting her whenever necessary. So, the money she had given to her nephew served her in good stead decades later when she was older. It provided her support when she fell ill, was hospitalized, and underwent medical treatment until she died. The money I had sent to my parents covered all her expenses, including her post-death expenses. All my aunt did was give some pocket money to a child, but such a simple act is indeed important.

It is difficult for family members or relatives to take care of their family members who they have lost touch with. It is not possible to take care of someone who has completely lost contact and whose whereabouts are unknown. Please know that as long as you believe and live by the "Three Happinesses" of Happiness Saving, Happiness Sharing, and Happiness Planting, someone will surely come to help you when you are in need. So, please do not be self-centered.

[Originally recorded in Japanese on June 30, 2016 at the Special Lecture Hall of Happy Science in Japan.]

Q2

Dialogue with a Young Man Suffering from Schizophrenia

QUESTIONER B

I have been diagnosed with a mental disorder called schizophrenia. I would like to ask you, what kinds of *kigan* (ritual prayer) and seminars should people with schizophrenia take to overcome it? How can they recover from this disorder? And what kind of mindset should they have? Please give us advice on these points.

Doctors sometimes create "believers"
by prescribing medicine

RYUHO OKAWA

Do you have an attending psychiatrist?

QUESTIONER B

Yes, I do.

RYUHO OKAWA

What does your psychiatrist say about how bad your condition is? Does he say it is serious or mild?

QUESTIONER B

I do not really know about that.

RYUHO OKAWA

As far as I can see, you are asking me questions in a rational manner and you seem to be a sound person, so I do not know why you are diagnosed with schizophrenia.

Maybe your psychiatrist has given you the wrong diagnosis. You seem quite normal to me.

QUESTIONER B

But I tend to lose my temper more easily than other people.

RYUHO OKAWA

Many people are like that.

QUESTIONER B

But I can actually become quite dangerous.

RYUHO OKAWA

So you become dangerous when you lose your temper? Is there anything else that you do?

QUESTIONER B

Other than this... Well, I get anxious about what other people are thinking about.

RYUHO OKAWA

That is normal. There is nothing wrong with that. It is normal for people to be conscious of what others are thinking.

QUESTIONER B

Really?

RYUHO OKAWA

Actually, people who cannot read the room should be the ones to worry. There is nothing wrong with those who are conscious of others.

QUESTIONER B

Actually, I am taking medicine for it...

RYUHO OKAWA

Doctors prescribe medicine because if they do not, people will not come back to their clinics or hospitals. So they are actually prescribing medicine to create "believers." Doctors tell their patients, "Come back when you run out of medicine." This way, hospitals are creating their believers.

**If you do not remember what you did,
your soul could have left your body**

RYUHO OKAWA

When you lose your temper, do you feel you have lost yourself for a moment?

QUESTIONER B

No, I do not.

RYUHO OKAWA

So you are aware.

QUESTIONER B

Yes.

The Miracle Power to Overcome Illness

RYUHO OKAWA

You are aware that you are in a rage.

QUESTIONER B

Yes, I am.

RYUHO OKAWA

Then, your condition is not that serious.

Some people do not remember what they did when they flew into a rage. They are unaware of the actions they take. These types of people are in a dangerous situation.

This is actually a spiritual matter. When people lose their memory, their souls are often separated from their physical bodies at that time. And while they are away, other spirits take over their body and say or do all kinds of bad things. That is the problem. Some people lose their temper and punch others but do not remember doing so. Others fly into a rage and set something on fire but they cannot recall doing it. Some lose their temper and stab someone with a knife but do not remember it at all. There are many cases like these. These kinds of people are also labeled as having an illness, but to tell the truth, this is a spiritual matter. Their souls easily leave their bodies, and as soon as they do, other spirits enter and occupy their bodies for a couple of hours of the day.

So even if you lose your temper, as long as you are yourself and are aware that you are angry, your condition is not so severe. You do not need to take it so seriously. I think you can heal naturally. When the doctor tells you that you have a certain illness, you will start to feel as if you are ill, but this is a kind of hypnotism. It is natural for people to be angry sometimes.

Establish yourself by learning the Truth and worldly knowledge, and protect yourself from evil spirits

RYUHO OKAWA

Do you get violent when you are in a rage?

QUESTIONER B

In the worst case, I feel like killing the other person.

RYUHO OKAWA

Killing?

QUESTIONER B

Yes.

RYUHO OKAWA

Well, we see many cases of people wanting to kill others in TV series and movies.

QUESTIONER B

If I were not a member of Happy Science, I may have committed a crime by now.

RYUHO OKAWA

I see. That is most probably due to the influence of evil spirits. If you are possessed by an evil spirit and you lose control of yourself, then you might end up committing a crime. So what you need to do is to protect yourself from evil spirits and prevent them from entering your body. Make sure to be connected to Happy Science through faith and accept the warm encouragement from the people around you. Then, try to develop a strong sense of self. You need to anchor some "weight" within yourself.

I usually teach about the importance of removing your ego and becoming selfless, but in the case of people like you, it is more important to establish the self first. Do not be empty-minded but instead, tell yourself, "This is the way I think. I believe this is the right way of thinking." In this way, have your own opinions and build a sense of self.

To build a self, first, you need knowledge of the Truth. You can gain this by reading my books. Another thing you need is knowledge and information about this world. According to worldly views, some things are considered strange and some things are considered right. You need to be able to make sound judgments based on these views. You will be in danger if you are too consumed by spiritual matters.

Schizophrenia is usually caused by spiritual influences

RYUHO OKAWA

In your case, I do not think you need to worry too much. "Schizophrenia" may sound like a serious illness, but it is just a name that doctors give to symptoms that they do not understand. In fact, symptoms like yours are usually caused by spiritual influences. It is a matter of whether or not you can take control of the spiritual influence that may be exerted on you. This ability differs from person to person.

As Happy Science members become spiritually receptive by attending our seminars regularly at our facilities, some of them may start to hear the voices of spirits or find their bodies moving on their own. But what is essential is how much you can be in control of yourself after experiencing such spiritual phenomena.

When an evil spirit approaches you, you need to make sure you are not controlled or used by it to fulfill its desires. To avoid being controlled by an evil spirit, you need to firmly establish yourself. You should also find something that you can cultivate yourself with, an activity that will allow you to check your progress. And you must continue doing it. Do you have anything you are good at or you like to do?

QUESTIONER B

I am fully devoted to Buddha's Truth.

RYUHO OKAWA

That is wonderful. Well, your doctor may say you are ill, but I do not think it is a serious problem. In your case, I do not think you are ill. Just make an effort to control your anger and stay calm and peaceful. Let us make efforts together. There are many things in this world that make us angry. Indeed there are, but we can develop the ability to control our anger, just as we can develop our muscles by training.

Tell yourself, "I'm getting better, little by little"

QUESTIONER B

I am not sure if this is a side effect of the medicine I take, but when I am working, I get tired very quickly.

RYUHO OKAWA

I get tired when I work, too [*laughs*]. What kind of work do you do?

QUESTIONER B

I work at a social welfare facility, but I want to work for a private company. So I wrote this down in my prayer form when I took the "Sacred Ritual to Realize Your Heart's True Desire." But my wish has not come true yet...

RYUHO OKAWA

What do you do specifically?

QUESTIONER B

It is a simple task, like the ones you can do at home.

RYUHO OKAWA

Well, you will not be able to do difficult tasks all of a sudden, so you must strongly wish that your performance at work will improve little by little. Believe and tell yourself that every day, you are getting better and better at doing your job. You should use autosuggestion. Tell yourself, "Every day, I am getting better and better at doing my work. Every day, I am gaining skills to do higher-level work. I will definitely be able to do a good job." You will not be able to improve your skills instantly. If you suddenly take up work that comes with heavy responsibility, you may become spiritually unstable again.

I think it is a matter of how much you can be in control of spiritual matters. So I will give your guardian spirit a scolding. He is probably taking a nap. I will tell him to work properly. What is your name?

QUESTIONER B

My name is B.

RYUHO OKAWA

All right. "The guardian spirit of Mr. B, do your job! Work properly. Do your job. If you are slacking off and taking a nap, I will punish you. I will not allow it!"

I have scolded your guardian spirit [*audience laughs*]. Please believe that you are improving little by little every day. Do not worry too much. Doctors will seldom tell you good things. Basically, the more patients with serious illnesses, the more money hospitals make. That is how they do their business. If you have a strong belief that you will get better, you will definitely get better. What you are experiencing is quite common in this world. It was a mistake that you went to the hospital. Hospitals will always diagnose you with an illness when you go there. Do not take your condition so seriously. You can still cure it by your own effort. So do not worry. You will be OK.

QUESTIONER B

Thank you very much.

[Originally recorded in Japanese on September 13, 2009 at Sagamihara Temple of Happy Science in Kanagawa, Japan.]

[Note: Questioner B's condition improved after this Q&A session. He continues to regularly attend Happy Science activities at his local temple.]

How to Cope with Dementia

QUESTIONER C

Recently, there have been more cases of dementia in younger people. I would like to know if there is any spiritual influence behind this trend. Also, could you please give advice to people who take care of a family member with dementia?

Dementia is not a problem of the soul
but of the physical body

RYUHO OKAWA

I am not well-versed in the medical data about dementia. What age group do you mean by "younger people"? I do not understand specifically which age group you have in mind, and I am not sure if there really is an increase in younger people with dementia. I do not know if there is medical proof of that nor do I know the statistics, so it is hard for me to say.

In any case, it is quite common for older people to go senile. This is the same as how cars break down after being used for a long time. A car will gradually wear out over the decades. It is in perfect condition in the beginning, but it will eventually wear out. Which part of the car goes bad first will depend on how you drive it. The screws might get loose, the car body might get damaged, the oil might leak, or the steering wheel might stop working. It is sad, but it cannot be helped. And if your car is damaged, you will not be able to run a race with it no matter how good a driver you are.

In the same way, the human body will deteriorate as you live for several decades. Your soul may remain healthy, but your body will wear out. This is inevitable as we live in this world. Not only humans but animals and insects also experience this. Their bodies will go bad as they get older. Animals get ill, too. Dogs and cats also show symptoms similar to dementia and when they age, they sometimes display odd behaviors as if they have gone senile. They contract various illnesses as well.

The same can be said of insects. Although the lifespan of rhino beetles is very short, their bodies still wither. For example, if it falls from a tree and hits its head when it is about to get caught, it will die much sooner. If one gets its leg caught on something and loses it, it will also die much earlier.

In this way, all living creatures with physical bodies in this world will reach a point where they cannot live to their full capacity. This is because physical bodies deteriorate over time. As one gets older, their body gradually declines. This corresponds to Aging and Illness in the Four Pains taught in Buddhism—which are birth, aging, illness, and death—and cannot be completely avoided.

Three secrets to stop you from going senile

Then, what are the secrets to prevent yourself from going senile as you age?

•Take care of your health

The general rule is to take care of your health. Have good routines as much as possible. You should also walk as much as you can because, as you age, your legs will get weaker first.

•Learn new information

People will likely go senile if they do not learn new information, so it is also important to acquire new knowledge. It is said that elderly people go senile quickly because nursing homes are usually built in the countryside with beautiful views. While these places are good environments for walking, which is an important factor, elderly people easily go senile if there is hardly any information they can acquire.

•Stay young at heart

You also need to stay young at heart. It is said that elderly women living in nursing homes feel younger and can think clearly when they wear makeup. This means that you need to have the will to live rather than just letting things wither away.

In short, you need to look after your own health and diet and stay young at heart by always taking an interest in something. These efforts will prevent you from going senile. But if your body nevertheless gets damaged and does not function well enough, you should learn to accept it.

Having a pet is one way to feel younger and rejuvenated

People can go senile earlier if they lose their reason to live at a young age. Even those in their 50s can go senile if they lose their motivation to live, for example, when their project abruptly ends and they have nothing else to do at work or when their children move out at an early age. I recommend such people to own a pet. A pet can be very good as a substitute for children, in a sense, because it is a living creature and it has various thoughts. By talking to your pet and taking care of it, you can feel rejuvenated.

I have a pet rabbit at home (as of 2001). It used to be a calm rabbit; when we held it in our arms, it would hold still. But, one summer, we took it with us to the mountains and let it run outside. After that, it became a little wild and violent. It dug holes, scratched things with its claws, and bit us. My family was saying that we could no longer keep it as a pet, but I came up with an idea and had the rabbit listen to the CD of my recitation of "The True Words Spoken By Buddha" (see p.160). Then, after two weeks, it became calm again. It stopped biting or scratching things with its claws and was spending most of the day in a "meditative state" [*audience laughs*]. It just lies on its back, showing its white belly and meditating like a Buddhist monk—or perhaps, more like a Taoist monk. I was amazed to see how "The True Words Spoken By Buddha" is effective on animals as well.

At any rate, you will be required to feed and clean up the mess by owning a living animal. If you do not want to do that, a robotic pet is also fine. There are various robotic pets now, like robotic dogs and robotic cats. People who do not like to have a living creature around can try owning a robotic pet. In any case, you need something to keep you stimulated.

Dementia can start in one's late 40s or 50s. When people lose motivation to live, they can quickly grow old and become senile. For example, their children may move out of the house and become independent or their children may die from an illness. Or, it may be that their business goes bankrupt and they have to close it down. When people lose their reason to live by such a turn of events, they may sometimes develop dementia. These people should find a new reason to live as they train their bodies and keep fit.

Elementary school students learn things through repetition

This is different from dementia, but people who are much younger can also be forgetful. Even elementary school children easily forget what they have learned at school. In fact, many children forget what they learned just the day before. They simply cannot remember. So they need to be taught the same thing repeatedly, again and again. Otherwise, they will not be able to retain what they learn. The elderly are not the only ones who are forgetful; elementary school children are also forgetful.

Most of them will not remember the things they learned a month ago, even if they studied them properly. Only extremely outstanding students can remember what they learn. To be blunt, elementary school students will forget the things they learned a week ago, three days ago, or even the day before. Once they learn something new, they will forget what they have learned previously.

School education is actually based on the assumption that students cannot retain what they have learned. That is why teachers teach the same thing over and over again. For example, they spend a whole year teaching addition or multiplication. It takes a lot of patience to do this. Even when children learn how to do it, they will quickly forget it in about a month. To make sure they do not forget, you have to teach them the same thing repeatedly for a year, or sometimes two to three years. Indeed, adults tend to become forgetful as they age, but the same is true with children. Even so, regardless of your age, you can develop a better memory through training.

Discard old information to take in something new

Once your memory capacity reaches its limit, you will not be able to remember any more than that. This is natural. Just like a computer, everyone has a limit to the amount of information they can store. So you need to forget some of the information you retained and replace it with something more important. The only thing you can do is delete what is unnecessary and take in what you must remember. You need to discard the useless knowledge and dedicate your memory capacity to things you need now or in the near future. Delete unnecessary information from your memory. Then, you will have less stress when trying to remember new things. You cannot remember everything even if you try.

Since I have given numerous lectures, many people probably cannot remember everything that I taught. So what you can do is to prioritize the lectures that are most important to you and listen to them first.

You can take this approach. If you have forgotten the content of one of my lectures, you can listen to it again by playing the lecture CD or you can watch the lecture DVD. If you have forgotten it after listening to it five times, then listen to it again after a while. Repetition is the only way to remember things. This is the same for children as it is for elderly people. Older people who remember my lectures for years just by listening to them once are exceptionally intelligent.

Recently, I saw my children watching an old lecture of mine. Sometimes, I, myself, am surprised at how good of a lecture I gave. I thought to myself, "Oh, when did I give this lecture? Seems like I used to say good things back then as well." [*Laughs*.] If I am not careful, I might even give the same lecture without realizing it. If people call me senile for that, I would not be able to deny it. But this would show how many lectures I have given.

To produce something new, you must discard old information. Otherwise, this is impossible. When you add new information to your memory, old information will fade away. So when you remember something new, you will naturally forget some of the old things.

In my case, I forget some of the things I talked about in my past lectures so that I can give a new one. If I remember everything that I said, my mind will be all jumbled up with information. My lectures are recorded and are later made into CDs or DVDs and are also compiled into books, so I do not need to remember them all. That is why I can set them aside and cheerfully move on to giving a new lecture. It is convenient that the lectures are printed in books or recorded on CDs and DVDs because you can review them anytime you want.

Even if I were asked to give the same lecture I gave one year ago, I do not think I would be able to. I do not remember everything that I said in every lecture, though I remember the important points. If I were to give a lecture under the same title now, I would probably talk about something completely different. This is how things are.

There is a limit to how much people can remember things. So, try to distinguish what is important from what is not, and tell yourself that it is all right to forget the trivial things. But you must repeatedly learn and remember the important things. This is the only way to remember them. When you become aware of your capacity, discard the things that are unnecessary now. In your bookshelves or on your desk, leave only what you can digest right now and keep everything else out of sight. You can read or look at it later on when you have a chance.

Be selective in remembering daily news

Another point to keep in mind is that using your brain too much can wear you out. There are many newspapers and TV channels available, but they all practically report the same news. I read six or seven different newspapers every day, and I find that 70 to 80 percent of the news covered in all newspapers talks about the same thing. I do not want to read them all, but since they touch on slightly different topics, I read them anyway.

This means I will be reading six or seven articles on similar topics, such as a murder case, an economic downturn, or a company's bankruptcy. But if I remembered all the details, that would be quite troublesome. So it is important *not* to remember some information even if you read it. Just forget it by the next day. You must be selective in what you memorize and be able to wisely delete some of your memory. Delete unpleasant information as quickly as possible. You will have a tough time if you remember it all.

Only detectives and criminals who are on the run need to know specific information like the year and date of a murder case. Other people do not need to know that. Even just remembering where the murder happened will give you an unpleasant feeling. Mystery fans may be interested in how the murder took place, but this is unnecessary information for the majority of people. Regardless, the news gives you a detailed description of how the incident happened, such as where the bloodstains and weapons were found. Do not remember these things. Forget them. Simply memorizing information is not all that important. You should also erase unnecessary information from your memory.

Let unhappy memories "evaporate" and repeatedly recall happy ones

The same can be said of happy and unhappy memories. People who remember unhappy memories and forget about happy ones tend to feel more miserable. At times, you can not avoid unhappy experiences but try to let those memories "evaporate" as soon as possible. Try to recall happy memories again and again instead, much like how cows chew the cud. If you do so, you will be able to feel that you have always been happy.

It is better to forget unhappy incidents swiftly and as soon as possible, even a day sooner. In this sense, going senile could be a happy thing. Some people will have to continue to suffer unless they go senile. Since there is a limit to how much memory a brain can store, it is possible to forget about unpleasant or bad memories of the past. You may get flashbacks once in a while, but it is a good thing that you can forget about them in your daily life.

You do not need to finish reading books that are not worth the time

I have always been confident in my brain capacity, but I have had times when I lost my memory about certain things. I really felt like a child who had lost his memory. Since 1991, I have been reading over 1,000 books a year. However, I noticed that as I read more and more books, some information would slip from my memory. It seems that storing too much information in the brain's "library" can make it difficult to retrieve it. This is because too much information is piled up one after the other. In other cases, some information disappears from the memory over time. Through this experience, I realized that just reading book after book is not necessarily a good thing.

It is better to narrow down the books you read and focus on reading the important ones that are worth reading, deeply and repeatedly. As you read them four or five times, the contents will become your own knowledge and power, which will then enable you to say meaningful things to others. But if you read too many journalistic books or popular books that only deal with fleeting information, not only will the contents quickly fade from your memory but will also mess up your brain and make you lose the important information. To prevent this from happening, you need to refrain from taking in too much trivial information or make an effort not to remember it. I read many things because I need them for my work, but afterward, I try to erase what I think is unnecessary. It is important to have the ability to judge whether something is necessary or not.

Even if you buy a book, there are times when you need to make an effort *not* to read it. Sometimes you cannot judge a book unless you buy and read it. But once you start reading it and find that the ideas in the book are doubtful, mistaken, or worthless, you need to stop reading it. If you continue reading it nevertheless and take in all the information, the knowledge you gained from other important books will fade. You need to be aware of your brain capacity and be selective about what information to remember.

In the modern age,
it is essential to select the necessary information

Children, as well as middle-aged people, can be forgetful. Young people also forget things. If they did not, they would not get terrible scores on their exams. Even young people have a limit to how much they can remember, so they need to be more considerate of themselves on this point. If they use too much energy on remembering trifling matters, it will drain their energy and they may end up behaving and thinking like someone who has gone senile.

In the modern age, information is overflowing, so be selective about what information you take in and intentionally erase the trivial. You need to make an effort to forget some information and remember only what is important through repeated learning.

After all, as we are living beings, going senile is something we cannot avoid. Even animals go senile. But there are both negative and positive sides to it. Some people can become happy by forgetting things. Perhaps this is one of the reasons why many elderly people go senile. Those who have had a lot of painful experiences may sometimes become happier by going senile. It seems those who go senile at an early age compared to others are those who retain many memories that they do not want to remember. In this way, going senile can be another form of happiness.

[Originally recorded in Japanese on October 17, 2001 at Happy Science General Headquarters in Tokyo, Japan.]

Afterword

There are certainly ways to deal with illness. The key is to take enough nutrients every day, exercise regularly, and switch from a stressful lifestyle to a calm one where you do not take things to heart so easily. Having pure, indomitable faith will also work to enhance your immunity. Moreover, you need to study Buddha's Truth to maintain a state of mind that wards off devils and evil spirits.

Sometimes, a miracle that completely overturns the "doctor's prophecy" will happen. At such times, take it as a message that you have a mission and responsibility toward many people. God will, of course, want to save altruistic people over egotistical people.

Be a big-hearted person who can forgive and love others. When you become a person who can gain some kind of enlightenment even through illness, you shall be granted the Miracle Power.

Ryuho Okawa
Master & CEO of Happy Science Group
February 13, 2018

Testimonies of Miraculous Recovery from Illnesses

Many Happy Science members have experienced miraculous recovery from their illnesses as they led a life of faith. Here, we will share some of their experiences.

✦ CASE 1

A toe grew back after necrosis

A.Y. (50s, female) from Aichi Prefecture, Japan

Last year, my husband, who had been suffering from diabetes, had necrosis on his left ring toe. The doctor suggested that he amputate everything below his knee. So he took Happy Science kigans (ritual prayers) such as "Prayer to Eradicate Illnesses." He also practiced self-reflection and deepened his gratitude toward the Lord and the people who had supported and helped him in the past.

Then, his ring toe, which he had lost due to necrosis, gradually grew back. Even its skin color and nail were restored. With three months of hospitalization and a month of follow-up visits—in total of about four months—the toe was fully restored to its original form. He no longer needed to amputate his leg. The doctor was shocked and said that it was absolutely unbelievable.

Now, my husband can walk on his feet without a wheelchair or a walking stick.

CASE *2*

Fully recovered from a bedridden state

F.W. (40s, female) from Aichi Prefecture, Japan

I used to have a chronic illness called lumbar spondylolisthesis. A few years ago, it took a turn for the worse and I became bedridden and required care. Every time I moved my body, I felt a sharp pain.

My aunt, who is a Happy Science believer, recommended that I practice self-reflection and deepen my gratitude, so I practiced them even as I suffered in pain. Then surprisingly, my pain gradually faded, and about a month later, I was able to visit Hakone Shoja.

When I was praying in the prayer hall at the shoja, I had a surprising experience: I felt as if a shining staff had pierced my spine. Right after that, I no longer needed crutches to walk. I also took the kigan, "Prayer for Doubling Our Health" on that day.

Since then, I have been able to lead a normal, healthy life.

To read more testimonies from members, check out our monthly magazines. Contact your nearest Happy Science location for more details.

Seminars and kigans to receive the healing light from heaven and help you overcome illnesses

Happy Science offers various kigans, or ritual prayers, that will help you get back on your feet and regain a healthy life. Here are just a few of them.

Kigans at Shoja

Prayer to Receive Healing Power

Through this prayer, those who believe in the infinite power of God that forgives all sins and saves all people will be given the healing light. People will be able to recover from any illnesses.

Held at shojas around the world.

Prayer to Regenerate Function
—Special Spiritual Guidance by God Ophealis—

Through this prayer, you will receive the miraculous power from God Ophealis to regenerate and recuperate any failing of bodily function. God Ophealis is the origin of the resurrection myth in ancient Egypt.

Held at shojas around the world.

Prayer for Cancer Cells to Disappear

In this prayer, you will ask God to forgive you of your mistaken thoughts and sins committed in your past lives, that are the cause of cancer cells. The infinite Light of God will flow into your body and make all cancer cells disappear.

Held at shojas around the world.

Super Strong Prayer for Healing Illness
—Special Spiritual Guidance by Jesus Christ—

This prayer will vanish the root cause of your illness such as your internal conflict, karma from past lives, and sense of guilt that has been built up in your mind. Light will shine upon all illnesses and good health will be established.

Held at shojas around the world and local branches outside Japan.

Prayer for Doubling Our Health

This prayer is guided by God Ophealis, who has tremendous spiritual power. This miraculous and mystical kigan will remove all kinds of obstacles and enhance your health twice as much.

Held at shojas around the world and local branches outside Japan.

Powerful Healing Prayer to Counter Hay Fever

In this prayer, you will receive guidance from God Ophealis, the Great Mystic God. You will ask for protection from any pollen that makes you ill or unwell, and wish to enhance your health significantly.

Held at shojas and local branches around the world.

*Shoja is a Happy Science facility where you can take kigans and seminars. It is a holy place where heavenly light pours down abundantly. Being embraced by the peaceful light, you will be able to find your true self full of energy. For details, please contact your nearest Happy Science location on pp. 162-163.

The kigans introduced in this section are available as of July 2024.

Seminars at Shoja

Special Koan Seminar on Miraculous Ways to Conquer Cancer

This seminar is recommended to all who wish to receive the miraculous power of resurrection.

Held at shojas and local branches around the world.

Gratitude to Parents Reflection Seminar

In this seminar, you will look back on your life since childhood, and reflect on and deepen your gratitude for the love your parents gave you.

Held at shojas around the world and local branches outside Japan.

Monthly Prayers Conducted at Local Temple and Branch

✦ **Prayer for Recovery from Illness**
✦ **Prayer for Health**

Other kigans are also available. Please contact your nearest local branch or shoja for details.

The kigans introduced in this section are available as of July 2024.

ABOUT THE AUTHOR

Founder and CEO of Happy Science Group.

Ryuho Okawa was born on July 7th 1956, in Tokushima, Japan. After graduating from the University of Tokyo with a law degree, he joined a Tokyo-based trading house. While working at its New York headquarters, he studied international finance at the Graduate Center of the City University of New York. In 1981, he attained Great Enlightenment and became aware that he is El Cantare with a mission to bring salvation to all humankind.

In 1986, he established Happy Science. It now has members in 170 countries across the world, with more than 700 branches and temples as well as 10,000 missionary houses around the world.

He has given over 3,500 lectures (of which more than 150 are in English) and published over 3,150 books (of which more than 600 are Spiritual Interview Series), and many of which are translated into 42 languages. Along with *The Laws of the Sun* and *The Laws of Hell*, many of the books have become best sellers or million sellers. To date, Happy Science has produced 27 movies under his supervision. He has given the original story and concept and is also the Executive Producer. He has also composed music and written lyrics for over 450 pieces.

Moreover, he is the Founder of Happy Science University and Happy Science Academy (Junior and Senior High School), Founder and President of the Happiness Realization Party, Founder and Honorary Headmaster of Happy Science Institute of Government and Management, Founder of IRH Press Co., Ltd., and the Chairperson of NEW STAR PRODUCTION Co., Ltd. and ARI Production Co., Ltd.

BOOKS BY RYUHO OKAWA

Healing Books

Words to Read in Times of Illness

Hardcover • 136 pages • $17.95
ISBN: 978-1-958655-07-8 (Sep. 15, 2023)

Ryuho Okawa has written 100 Healing Messages to comfort the souls of those going through any illness. When we are ill, it is an ideal time for us to contemplate recent and past events, as well as our relationship with the people around us. It is a chance for us to take inventory of our emotions and thoughts.

Healing from Within

Life-Changing Keys to Calm, Spiritual, and Healthy Living

Paperback • 208 pages • $15.95
ISBN:978-1-942125-18-1 (Jun. 30, 2017)

None of us wants to become sick, but why is it that we can't avoid illness in life? Is there a meaning behind illness? In this book, author Ryuho Okawa reveals the true causes and remedies for various illnesses that modern medicine doesn't know how to heal. Building a happier and healthier life starts with believing in the power of our mind and understanding the relationship between mind and body.

Worry-Free Living

Let Go of Stress and Live in Peace and Happiness

Hardcover • 192 pages • $16.95
ISBN: 978-1-942125-51-8 (May 15, 2019)

The wisdom Ryuho Okawa shares in this book about facing problems in human relationships, financial hardships, and other life stresses will help you change how you look at and approach life's worries and problems for the better. Let this book be your guide to finding precious meaning in all your life's problems, gaining inner growth and practicing inner happiness and spiritual growth.

Healing Power

The True Mechanism of Mind and Illness

Paperback • 190 pages • $14.95
ISBN: 979-8-88737-048-4 (Feb. 18, 2016)

This book describes the relationship between the mind and illness, and provides you with hints to restore your mental and physical health. By reading this book, you can find tips on how to heal your body from illnesses such as cancer, heart disease, allergy, skin disease, dementia, psychiatric disorders, and atopy. You will gain the miraculous power of healing.

El Cantare Trilogy

The Laws Series is an annual volume of books that are comprised of Ryuho Okawa's lectures that function as universal guidance to all people. They are of various topics that were given in accordance with the changes that each year brings. *The Laws of the Sun*, the first publication of the Laws Series, ranked in the annual best-selling list in Japan in 1994. Since then, the Laws Series' titles have ranked in the annual best-selling list every year for more than two decades, setting socio-cultural trends in Japan and around the world. The first three Laws Series are *The Laws of the Sun*, *The Golden Laws*, and *The Laws of Eternity*.

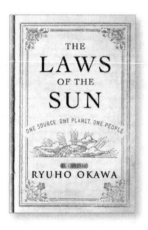

The Laws of the Sun

One Source, One Planet, One People

Paperback • 288 pages • $15.95
ISBN: 978-1-942125-43-3 (Oct. 15, 2018)

IMAGINE IF YOU COULD ASK GOD why He created this world and what spiritual laws He used to shape us—and everything around us. If we could understand His designs and intentions, we could discover what our goals in life should be and whether our actions move us closer to those goals or farther away. At a young age, a spiritual calling prompted Ryuho Okawa to outline what he innately understood to be universal truths for all humankind. In *The Laws of the Sun*, Okawa outlines these laws of the universe and provides a road map for living one's life with greater purpose and meaning. In this powerful book, Ryuho Okawa reveals the transcendent nature of consciousness and the secrets of our multidimensional universe and our place in it. By understanding the different stages of love and following the Buddhist Eightfold Path, he believes we can speed up our eternal process of development. *The Laws of the Sun* shows the way to realize true happiness—a happiness that continues from this world through the other.

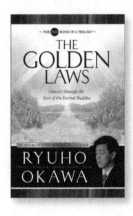

The Golden Laws

History through the Eyes of
the Eternal Buddha

E-book • 204 pages • $13.99
ISBN: 978-1-941779-82-8 (Sep. 24, 2015)

Throughout history, Great Guiding Spirits have been present on Earth in both the East and the West at crucial points in human history to further our spiritual development. *The Golden Laws* reveals how the Divine Plan has been unfolding on Earth, and outlines 5,000 years of the secret history of humankind. Once we understand the true course of history, through past, present, and into the future, we cannot help but become aware of the significance of our spiritual mission in the present age.

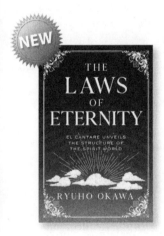

The Laws of Eternity

El Cantare Unveils the Structure of the Spirit World

Paperback • 200 pages • $17.95
ISBN: 978-1-958655-16-0 (May. 15, 2024)

This book reveals the eternal mysteries and the ultimate secrets of Earth's Spirit Group that have been covered by the veil of legends and myths. Encountering the long-hidden Eternal Truths that are revealed for the first time in human history will change the way you live your life now.

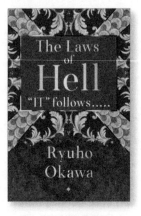

The Laws of Hell

"IT" follows.....

Paperback • 264 pages • $17.95
ISBN: 978-1-958655-04-7 (May 1, 2023)

Whether you believe it or not, the Spirit World and hell do exist. Currently, the Earth's population has exceeded 8 billion, and unfortunately, 1 in 2 people are falling to hell.

This book is a must-read at a time like this since more and more people are unknowingly heading to hell; the truth is, new areas of hell are being created, such as 'internet hell' and 'hell on earth.' Also, due to the widespread materialism, there is a sharp rise in the earthbound spirits wandering around Earth because they have no clue about the Spirit World.

To stop hell from spreading and to save the souls of all human beings, Ryuho Okawa has compiled vital teachings in this book. This publication marks his 3,100th book and is the one and only comprehensive Truth about the modern hell.

Recommended Books

The Truth about Spiritual Phenomena

Life's Q&A with El Cantare

Paperback • 232 pages • $17.95
ISBN: 978-1-958655-0-92 (Oct. 27, 2023)

These are the records of Ryuho Okawa's answers to 26 questions related to spiritual phenomena and mental health, which were conducted live during his early public lectures with the audience. With his great spiritual ability, he revealed the unknown spiritual Truth behind the spiritual phenomena.

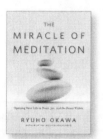

The Miracle of Meditation

Opening Your Life to Peace, Joy, and the Power Within

Paperback • 207 pages • $15.95
ISBN: 978-1-942125-09-9 (Nov. 1, 2016)

This book introduces various types of meditation, including calming meditation, purposeful meditation, reading meditation, reflective meditation, and meditation to communicate with heaven. Through reading and practicing meditation in this book, we can experience the miracle of meditation, which is to start living a life of peace, happiness, and success.

An Unshakable Mind

How to Overcome Life's Difficulties

Paperback • 180 pages • $17.95
ISBN:978-1-942125-91-4 (Nov. 30, 2023)

This book will guide you to build the genuine self-confidence necessary to shape a resilient character and withstand life's turbulence. Author Ryuho Okawa breaks down the cause of life's difficulties and provides solutions to overcome them from the spiritual viewpoint of life based on the laws of the mind.

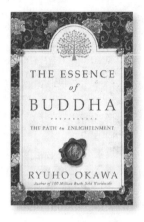

The Essence of Buddha

The Path to Enlightenment

Paperback • 208 pages • $14.95
ISBN: 978-1-942125-06-8 (Oct. 1, 2016)

In this book, Ryuho Okawa imparts in simple and accessible language his wisdom about the essence of Shakyamuni Buddha's philosophy of life and enlightenment—teachings that have been inspiring people all over the world for over 2,500 years. By offering a new perspective on core Buddhist thoughts that have long been cloaked in mystique, Okawa brings these teachings to life for modern people. *The Essence of Buddha* distills a way of life that anyone can practice to achieve a life of self-growth, compassionate living, and true happiness.

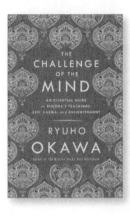

The Challenge of the Mind

An Essential Guide to Buddha's Teachings:
Zen, Karma and Enlightenment

Paperback • 208 pages • $16.95
ISBN: 978-1-942125-45-7 (Nov. 15, 2018)

In this book, Ryuho Okawa explains essential
Buddhist tenets and how to put them into
practice. Enlightenment is not just an abstract
idea but one that everyone can experience to
some extent. Okawa offers a solid basis of reason
and an intellectual understanding of Buddhist
concepts. By applying these basic principles to
our lives, we can direct our minds to higher
ideals and create a bright future for ourselves
and others.

The Challenge of Enlightenment

Now, Here, the New Dharma Wheel Turns

Paperback • 380 pages • $17.95
ISBN: 978-1-942125-92-1 (Dec. 20, 2022)

Buddha's teachings, a reflection of his eternal
wisdom, are like a bamboo pole used to change
the course of your boat in the rapid stream of
the great river called life. By reading this book,
your mind becomes clearer, learns to savor
inner peace, and it will empower you to make
profound life improvements.

Words of Wisdom Series

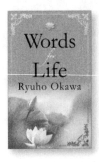

Words for Life

Paperback • 136 pages • $15.95
ISBN: 979-8-88737-089-7 (Mar. 16, 2023)

Ryuho Okawa has written over 3,150 books on various topics. To help readers find the teachings that are beneficial for them out of the extensive teachings, the author has written 100 phrases and put them together. Inside you will find words of wisdom that will help you improve your mindset and lead you to live a meaningful and happy life.

Words for Building Character

Paperback • 140 pages • $15.95
ISBN: 979-8-88737-091-0 (Jun. 21, 2023)

When your life comes to an end, what you can bring with you to the other world is your enlightenment, in other words, the character that you build in this lifetime. If you can read, relish, and truly understand the meaning of these religious phrases, you will be able to attain happiness that transcends this world and the next.

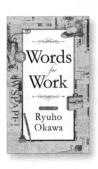

Words for Work

Paperback • 140 pages • $15.95
ISBN: 979-8-88737-090-3 (Jul. 20, 2023)

Through his personal experiences at work, Okawa has created these phrases regarding philosophies and practical wisdom about work. This book will be of great use to you throughout your career. Every day you can contemplate and gain tips on how to better your work as well as deepen your insight into company management.

MUSIC BY RYUHO OKAWA

A song celebrating Lord God / With Savior

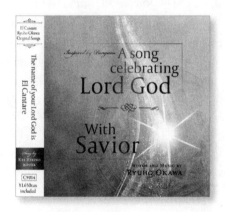

Words & Music by Ryuho Okawa

1. A song celebrating Lord God—Renewal ver.
2. With Savior —Renewal ver.
3. A song celebrating Lord God— Renewal ver. (Instrumental)
4. With Savior —Renewal ver. (Instrumental)
5. With Savior —Renewal ver. (Instrumental with chorus)

WHO IS EL CANTARE?

El Cantare means "the Light of the Earth." He is the Supreme God of the Earth who has been guiding humankind since the beginning of Genesis, and He is the Creator of the universe. He is whom Jesus called Father and Muhammad called Allah, and is *Ame-no-Mioya-Gami*, Japanese Father God. Different parts of El Cantare's core consciousness have descended to Earth in the past, once as Alpha and another as Elohim. His branch spirits, such as Shakyamuni Buddha and Hermes, have descended to Earth many times and helped to flourish many civilizations. To unite various religions and to integrate various fields of study in order to build a new civilization on Earth, a part of the core consciousness has descended to Earth as Master Ryuho Okawa.

Alpha is a part of the core consciousness of El Cantare who descended to Earth around 330 million years ago. Alpha preached Earth's Truths to harmonize and unify Earth-born humans and space people who came from other planets.

Elohim is a part of the core consciousness of El Cantare who descended to Earth around 150 million years ago. He gave wisdom, mainly on the differences between light and darkness, good and evil.

Ame-no-Mioya-Gami (Japanese Father God) is the Creator God and the Father God who appears in the ancient literature, *Hotsuma Tsutae*. It is believed that He descended on the foothills of Mt. Fuji about 30,000 years ago and built the Fuji dynasty, which is the root of the Japanese civilization. With justice as the central pillar, Ame-no-Mioya-Gami's teachings spread to ancient civilizations of other countries in the world.

Shakyamuni Buddha was born as a prince into the Shakya clan in India around 2,600 years ago. When he was 29 years old, he renounced the world and sought enlightenment. He later attained Great Enlightenment and founded Buddhism.

Hermes is one of the 12 Olympian gods in Greek mythology, but the spiritual Truth is that he taught the teachings of love and progress around 4,300 years ago which became the origin of the current Western civilization. He is a hero who truly existed.

Ophealis was born in Greece around 6,500 years ago and was the leader who took an expedition to as far as Egypt. He is the God of miracles, prosperity, and arts, and is known as Osiris in Egyptian mythology.

Rient Arl Croud was born as a king of the ancient Incan Empire around 7,000 years ago and taught about the mysteries of the mind. In the heavenly world, he is responsible for the interactions that take place between various planets.

Thoth was an almighty leader who built the golden age of the Atlantic civilization around 12,000 years ago. In Egyptian mythology, he is known as God Thoth.

Ra Mu was a leader who built the golden age of the civilization of Mu around 17,000 years ago. As a religious leader and a politician, he ruled by uniting religion and politics.

ABOUT HAPPY SCIENCE

Happy Science is a religious group founded on the faith in El Cantare who is the God of the Earth, and the Creator of the universe. The essence of human beings is the soul that was created by God, and we all are children of God. God is our true parent, so in our souls we have a fundamental desire to "believe in God, love God, and get closer to God." And, we can get closer to God by living with God's Will as our own. In Happy Science, we call this the "Exploration of Right Mind." More specifically, it means to practice the Fourfold Path, which consists of "Love, Wisdom, Self-Reflection, and Progress."

Love: Love means "love that gives," or mercy. God hopes for the happiness of all people. Therefore, living with God's Will as our own means to start by practicing "love that gives."

Wisdom: God's love is boundless. It is important to learn various Truths in order to understand the heart of God.

Self-Reflection: Once you learn the heart of God and the difference between His mind and yours, you should strive to bring your own mind closer to the mind of God—that process is called self-reflection. Self-reflection also includes meditation and prayer.

Progress: Since God hopes for the happiness of all people, you should also make progress in your love, and make an effort to realize utopia in which everyone in your society, country, and eventually all humankind can become happy.

As we practice this Fourfold Path, our souls will advance toward God step by step. That is when we can attain real happiness—our souls' desire to get closer to God comes true.

In Happy Science, we conduct activities to make ourselves happy through belief in Lord El Cantare, and to spread this faith to the world and bring happiness to all. We welcome you to join our activities!

We hold events and activities to help you practice the Fourfold Path at our branches, temples, missionary centers and missionary houses

Love: We hold various volunteering activities. Our members conduct missionary work together as the greatest practice of love.

Wisdom: We offer our comprehensive collection of books of Truth, many of which are available online and at Happy Science locations. In addition, we offer numerous opportunities such as seminars or book clubs to learn the Truth.

Self-Reflection: We offer opportunities to polish your mind through self-reflection, meditation, and prayer. Many members have experienced improvement in their human relationships by changing their own minds.

Progress: We also offer seminars to enhance your power of influence. Because it is also important to do well at work to make society better, we hold seminars to improve your work and management skills.

"The True Words Spoken By Buddha"

"The True Words Spoken By Buddha" is an English sutra given directly from the spirit of Shakyamuni Buddha, who is a part of Master Ryuho Okawa's subconscious. The words in this sutra are not of a mere human being but are the words of God or Buddha sent directly from the ninth dimension, which is the highest realm of the Earth's Spirit World.

"The True Words Spoken By Buddha" is an essential sutra for us to connect and live with God or Buddha's Will as our own.

MEMBERSHIPS

MEMBERSHIP

If you would like to know more about Happy Science, please consider becoming a member. Those who pledge to believe in Lord El Cantare and wish to learn more can join us.

When you become a member, you will receive the following sutras: "The True Words Spoken By Buddha," "Prayer to the Lord" and "Prayer to Guardian and Guiding Spirits."

DEVOTEE MEMBER

If you would like to learn the teachings of Happy Science and walk the path of faith, become a Devotee member who pledges devotion to the Three Treasures, which are Buddha, Dharma, and Sangha. Buddha refers to Lord El Cantare, Master Ryuho Okawa. Dharma refers to Master Ryuho Okawa's teachings. Sangha refers to Happy Science. Devoting to the Three Treasures will let your Buddha nature shine, and you will enter the path to attain true freedom of the mind.

Becoming a devotee means you become Buddha's disciple. You will discipline your mind and act to bring happiness to society.

✉ EMAIL OR ☎ PHONE CALL
Please see the contact information page.

🛜 ONLINE member.happy-science.org/signup/ 🔍

CONTACT INFORMATION

Happy Science is a worldwide organization with branches and temples around the globe. For full details, visit happy-science.org. The following are some of our main Happy Science locations:

UNITED STATES AND CANADA

New York
79 Franklin St., New York, NY 10013, USA
Phone: 1-212-343-7972
Fax: 1-212-343-7973
Email: ny@happy-science.org
Website: happyscience-usa.org

New Jersey
66 Hudson St., #2R, Hoboken, NJ 07030, USA
Phone: 1-201-313-0127
Email: nj@happy-science.org
Website: happyscience-usa.org

Chicago
2300 Barrington Rd., Suite #400, Hoffman Estates, IL 60169, USA
Phone: 1-630-937-3077
Email: chicago@happy-science.org
Website: happyscience-usa.org

Florida
5208 8th St., Zephyrhills, FL 33542, USA
Phone: 1-813-715-0000
Fax: 1-813-715-0010
Email: florida@happy-science.org
Website: happyscience-usa.org

Atlanta
1874 Piedmont Ave., NE Suite 360-C Atlanta, GA 30324, USA
Phone: 1-404-892-7770
Email: atlanta@happy-science.org
Website: happyscience-usa.org

San Francisco
525 Clinton St.
Redwood City, CA 94062, USA
Phone & Fax: 1-650-363-2777
Email: sf@happy-science.org
Website: happyscience-usa.org

Los Angeles
1590 E. Del Mar Blvd., Pasadena, CA 91106, USA
Phone: 1-626-395-7775
Fax: 1-626-395-7776
Email: la@happy-science.org
Website: happyscience-usa.org

Orange County
16541 Gothard St. Suite 104 Huntington Beach, CA 92647
Phone: 1-714-659-1501
Email: oc@happy-science.org
Website: happyscience-usa.org

San Diego
7841 Balboa Ave. Suite #202 San Diego, CA 92111, USA
Phone: 1-626-395-7775
Fax: 1-626-395-7776
E-mail: sandiego@happy-science.org
Website: happyscience-usa.org

Hawaii
Phone: 1-808-591-9772
Fax: 1-808-591-9776
Email: hi@happy-science.org
Website: happyscience-usa.org

Kauai
3343 Kanakolu Street, Suite 5 Lihue, HI 96766, USA
Phone: 1-808-822-7007
Fax: 1-808-822-6007
Email: kauai-hi@happy-science.org
Website: happyscience-usa.org

Toronto

845 The Queensway
Etobicoke, ON M8Z 1N6, Canada
Phone: 1-416-901-3747
Email: toronto@happy-science.org
Website: happy-science.ca

Vancouver

#201-2607 East 49th Avenue,
Vancouver, BC, V5S 1J9, Canada
Phone: 1-604-437-7735
Fax: 1-604-437-7764
Email: vancouver@happy-science.org
Website: happy-science.ca

INTERNATIONAL

Tokyo

1-6-7 Togoshi, Shinagawa,
Tokyo, 142-0041, Japan
Phone: 81-3-6384-5770
Fax: 81-3-6384-5776
Email: tokyo@happy-science.org
Website: happy-science.org

London

3 Margaret St.
London, W1W 8RE United Kingdom
Phone: 44-20-7323-9255
Fax: 44-20-7323-9344
Email: eu@happy-science.org
Website: www.happyscience-uk.org

Sydney

516 Pacific Highway, Lane Cove North,
2066 NSW, Australia
Phone: 61-2-9411-2877
Fax: 61-2-9411-2822
Email: sydney@happy-science.org

Sao Paulo

Rua. Domingos de Morais 1154,
Vila Mariana, Sao Paulo SP
CEP 04010-100, Brazil
Phone: 55-11-5088-3800
Email: sp@happy-science.org
Website: happyscience.com.br

Jundiai

Rua Congo, 447, Jd. Bonfiglioli
Jundiai-CEP, 13207-340, Brazil
Phone: 55-11-4587-5952
Email: jundiai@happy-science.org

Seoul

74, Sadang-ro 27-gil,
Dongjak-gu, Seoul, Korea
Phone: 82-2-3478-8777
Fax: 82-2-3478-9777
Email: korea@happy-science.org

Taipei

No. 89, Lane 155, Dunhua N. Road,
Songshan District, Taipei City 105, Taiwan
Phone: 886-2-2719-9377
Fax: 886-2-2719-5570
Email: taiwan@happy-science.org

Taichung

No. 146, Minzu Rd., Central Dist.,
Taichung City 400001, Taiwan
Phone: 886-4-22233777
Email: taichung@happy-science.org

Kuala Lumpur

No 22A, Block 2, Jalil Link Jalan Jalil Jaya
2, Bukit Jalil 57000,
Kuala Lumpur, Malaysia
Phone: 60-3-8998-7877
Fax: 60-3-8998-7977
Email: malaysia@happy-science.org
Website: happyscience.org.my

Kathmandu

Kathmandu Metropolitan City,
Ward No. 15, Ring Road, Kimdol,
Sitapaila Kathmandu, Nepal
Phone: 977-1-537-2931
Email: nepal@happy-science.org

Kampala

Plot 877 Rubaga Road, Kampala
P.O. Box 34130 Kampala, UGANDA
Email: uganda@happy-science.org   163

ABOUT HAPPINESS REALIZATION PARTY

The Happiness Realization Party (HRP) was founded in May 2009 by Master Ryuho Okawa as part of the Happy Science Group. HRP strives to improve Japanese society, based on three basic political principles of "freedom, democracy, and faith," and let Japan promote individual and public happiness from Asia to the world as a leader nation.

1) Diplomacy and Security: Protecting Freedom, Democracy, and Faith of Japan and the World from China's Totalitarianism

Japan's current defense system is insufficient against China's expanding hegemony and the threat of North Korea's nuclear missiles. Japan, as the leader of Asia, must strengthen its defense power and promote strategic diplomacy together with the nations that share the values of freedom, democracy, and faith. Further, HRP aims to realize world peace under the leadership of Japan, a nation with the spirit of religious tolerance.

2) Economy: Early economic recovery through utilizing the "wisdom of the private sector"

The economy has been damaged severely since the outbreak of the novel coronavirus originated in China. Many companies have been forced into bankruptcy or out of business. What is needed for economic recovery now is not subsidies and regulations by the government, but policies that can utilize the "wisdom of the private sector."

For more information, visit en.hr-party.jp

HAPPY SCIENCE ACADEMY JUNIOR AND SENIOR HIGH SCHOOL

Happy Science Academy Junior and Senior High School is a boarding school founded with the goal of educating the future leaders of the world who can have a big vision, persevere, and take on new challenges.

Currently, there are two campuses in Japan; the Nasu Main Campus in Tochigi Prefecture, founded in 2010, and the Kansai Campus in Shiga Prefecture, founded in 2013.

Nasu Main Campus

Kansai Campus

HAPPY SCIENCE UNIVERSITY

THE FOUNDING SPIRIT AND THE GOAL OF EDUCATION

Based on the founding philosophy of the university, "Exploration of happiness and the creation of a new civilization," education, research and studies will be provided to help students acquire a deep understanding grounded in religious belief and advanced expertise with the objectives of producing "great talents of virtue" who can contribute in a broad-ranging way to serve Japan and the international society.

FACULTIES

Faculty of human happiness

Students in this faculty will pursue liberal arts from various perspectives with a multidisciplinary approach, explore and envision an ideal state of human beings and society.

Faculty of successful management

This faculty aims to realize successful management that helps organizations to create value and wealth for society and to contribute to the happiness and development of management and employees as well as society as a whole.

Faculty of future creation

Students in this faculty study subjects such as political science, journalism, performing arts and artistic expression, and explore and present new political and cultural models based on truth, goodness and beauty.

Faculty of future industry

This faculty aims to nurture engineers who can resolve various issues facing modern civilization from a technological standpoint and contribute to the creation of new industries of the future.

ABOUT IRH PRESS USA INC.

Founded in 2013, New York-based IRH Press USA, Inc. is the North American affiliate of IRH Press Co., Ltd., Japan. The Press exclusively publishes comprehensive titles on Spiritual Truth, religious enrichment, Buddhism, personal growth, and contemporary commentary by Ryuho Okawa, the author of more than 3,150 unique publications, with hundreds of millions of copies sold worldwide. For more information, visit Okawabooks.com.

Follow us on:

f Facebook: Okawa Books   🄾 Instagram: OkawaBooks

▶ Youtube: Okawa Books   🐦 Twitter: Okawa Books

𝓟 Pinterest: Okawa Books   𝓰 Goodreads: Ryuho Okawa

——— **NEWSLETTER** ———

To receive book-related news, promotions and events, please subscribe to our newsletter below.

🔗 irhpress.com/pages/subscribe

 ——— **AUDIO / VISUAL MEDIA** ———

YOUTUBE   **PODCAST**

Introduction of Ryuho Okawa's titles; topics ranging from self-help, current affairs, spirituality, religion, and the universe.